Y0-CAX-975

INTERFACT REFERENCE

THE BOOK AND DISK THAT WORK TOGETHER

ATLAS

PRINCETON ■ LONDON

What's in the book?

What's on the disk?

First, get your Interfact passport. Follow the instructions on screen. Then explore the interactive maps and use the Picture Index to discover fascinating facts about the world's animals, plants, peoples, and places. As you travel the globe, be sure to visit the capital cities—some of them feature fun activities and exciting adventures (see right).

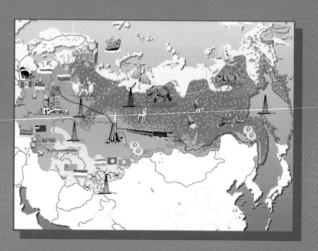

There are 16 interactive maps to explore.

Installing the Atlas CD-ROM

See page 48 for troubleshooting tips, system requirements, and helpline details.

Windows 95 or 98
The Atlas program should start automatically when you put the CD into your CD-ROM drive. If it does not, follow these instructions:
1. Put the CD into the CD drive
2. Double click on My Computer
3. Double click on the CD drive icon
4. Double click on the **Atlas** icon

Windows 3.1 or 3.11
1. Put the CD into the CD drive
2. Open File Manager
3. Double click on the CD drive icon
4. Double click on the **Atlas** icon

Macintosh
1. Put the CD into the CD drive
2. Double click on the **Atlas for Mac** icon

Power Macintosh
1. Put the CD into the CD drive
2. Double click on the **Atlas for Power Mac** icon

Virtual Globe
Take a closer look at the world using an amazing 3-D globe and answer rapid-fire questions on the continents.
Location: Sydney

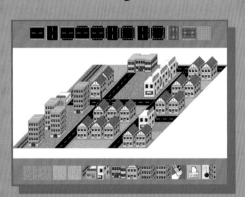

Find Agatha
Track down your long-lost Aunt Agatha using the book to solve the clues in the postcards she sends you.
Location: Washington, D.C.

World Class
Find the answers to all your questions about mapmaking and geography—this teacher is in a class of her own!
Location: Brasilia

Jigsaw Map
Pick up the pieces and put the world back together with these interactive jigsaws. Once each jigsaw is finished, click away to find out more!
Location: Tokyo

Map Maker
Create your own maps on screen. Print them out to keep or put your map-reading skills to the test and help Agatha find her missing purse.
Location: Cairo

Picture Index
There are over 400 interesting pictures in your Atlas. Use the Picture Index to find out more about each one—from Antarctic cod to desert lizards!
Location: Toolbar

*T*he Toolbar
The toolbar appears whenever you move the cursor to the right-hand edge of the screen.

 Click here to return to the main screen.

 Click here to go to the Picture Index.

 Click here to see activities completed.

 Click here to see your passport.

 Click here to use the note pad.

 Click here to go to the gift shop.

 Click here for help.

Click here to quit.

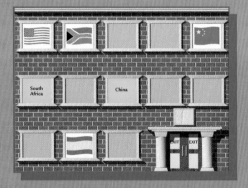

Windows on the World
A crazy memory challenge to test your knowledge. You'll be racing against the clock to match up countries with their capital cities, currencies, languages, and flags!
Location: Moscow

Around the World in 80 Days
Help Phileas and Passepartout navigate their way around the world. Visit more than 150 capital cities along the way.
Location: London

What is an atlas?

An atlas is a book of maps showing different parts of the world. Maps are small pictures of big places drawn from above. They can show somewhere as small as a village or as big as the world. You can use atlases and maps in all sorts of ways. They might show you how to find your way around, or tell you what a place is like.

1 One of the most difficult maps to draw is one showing all of the world. This is because the world is round, like a huge ball, but maps are flat. Imagine painting the world onto the skin of an orange.

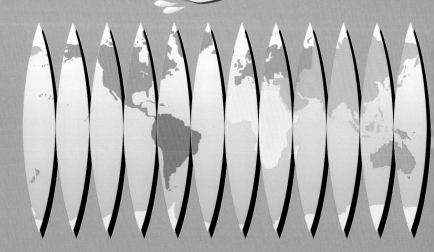

2 You could carefully peel the skin into segments.

3 Then you could lay the peel flat to make a map of the world.

ARCTIC OCEAN

Arctic Circle

NORTH AMERICA

EUROPE

ASIA

PACIFIC OCEAN

ATLANTIC OCEAN

AFRICA

Equator

INDIAN OCEAN

SOUTH AMERICA

AUSTRALIA

Antarctic Circle

ANTARCTICA

4 Mapmakers fill the gaps by stretching some parts of the map and shrinking others.

On this map, you can see that more than half of the Earth is covered by four big oceans. The rest of the Earth is divided into seven huge areas of land, called continents. There are also three imaginary lines on the map. The equator circles the Earth's center. The Arctic Circle is at the top of the Earth and the Antarctic Circle is at the bottom.

Different kinds of maps show different amounts of detail, but most maps show places much smaller than they really are.

1 This is a picture of a house on the corner of Park Street, which runs through a seaside town. You can see the hedge around the house, the tree outside and some of the street, but you cannot see the town or the sea because the picture is not big enough to show all these details.

2 This map shows Park Street from above. It shows less detail but a bigger area than before. Can you spot the house on the corner? Here, Park Street measures 4 inches (10cm), but it is really 1 mile (1km) long. This means that on the map every 4 inches (10cm) is the same as 1 mile (1km) in the real place. This is called *scale*.

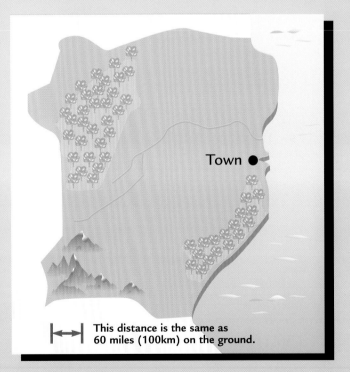

This distance is the same as 60 miles (100km) on the ground.

3 This map shows a bigger area than the last map because it has a smaller scale. It shows all of the town. You cannot see the houses or all the streets, but you can see Park Street. On this map, Park Street is 2 inches (5cm) long. This means every 2 inches (5cm) on the map is the same as 1 mile (1km) in the real place.

4 This map shows the country where the town is found. The town is shown as a dot. The scale bar tells you that $3/8$ inch (1cm) on the map is the same as 60 miles (100km) in the real place. In this atlas, each map has a different scale and scale bar. On pages 10-11 you can see all the whole world at the same scale.

Hot and cold

Around the world, there are different patterns of weather called climates. The climate of a country depends on where it is in the world. It is always hot near the equator and cold near the North and South Poles. On each map in this atlas, you will find a locator globe, showing you where countries and continents are in the world. The globe has arrows pointing to the four directions— north, south, east and west.

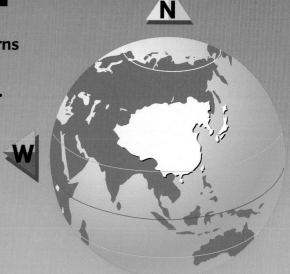

The sun warms all the countries in the world, but shines more strongly on some than others. These countries have the warmest weather. Around the world, the weather also changes at different times of year.

Arctic Circle

Around the North and South Poles, the sun is never high in the sky and shines weakly, so the land is always cold, especially in winter.

Tropic of Cancer

Near the equator, the sun shines strongest and directly from above. Here the climate is hot, with wet and dry seasons.

Equator

Above and below the equator, there are two imaginary lines called the Tropic of Cancer and the Tropic of Capricorn. Countries between the tropics and the North and South Poles have warm summers and cold winters.

Tropic of Capricorn

Different climates suit particular kinds of plants, and make different types of land for animals and people to live in. If a place has a rainy climate, lots of plants grow. If the climate is dry, fewer and different plants grow.

On the map below and the maps in this atlas, different types of land are shown by small pictures, called symbols, and colors. These photographs show you what the land really looks like.

Usually, the poles are icy cold. In summer, a few small plants grow around the Arctic.

Deciduous forests grow in cool areas. The trees lose their leaves in autumn.

Evergreen trees stay green all year. Evergreen forests grow in cold places.

Grassland includes tropical savanna (seen here), farmland and flat plains, called pampas.

Only the toughest plants and animals are able to survive in dry deserts.

Thick, green rainforests grow where it is warm and wet all year.

Few plants grow on rocky mountains, which are often covered in snow.

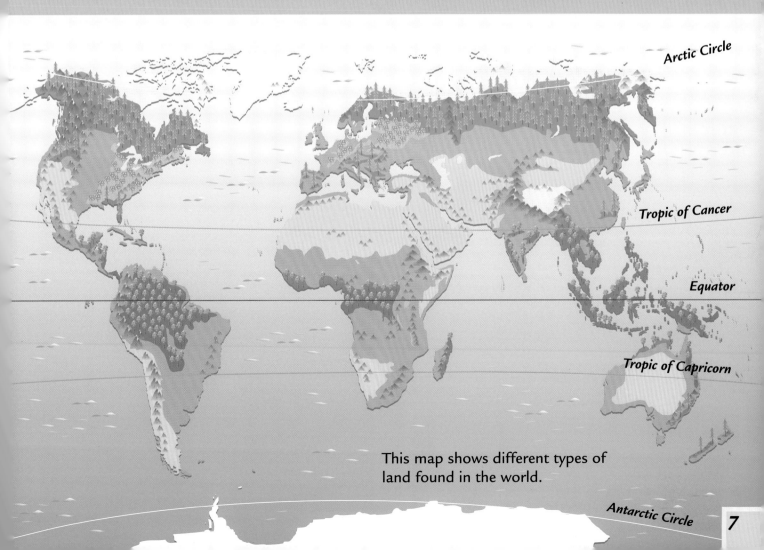

Arctic Circle

Tropic of Cancer

Equator

Tropic of Capricorn

This map shows different types of land found in the world.

Antarctic Circle

About this atlas

The maps in this atlas can tell you an enormous amount about the places they show. Look carefully at the pictures to find out more.

Crops grow all over the world. Look out for wheat, rice, fruit and vegetables. You may see coffee, tea and sugar cane, too.

Each country is run from a capital city. These are shown by the flag of the country and a star.

Some buildings are shown on the maps. You may see a famous monument, an old ruin or a type of home.

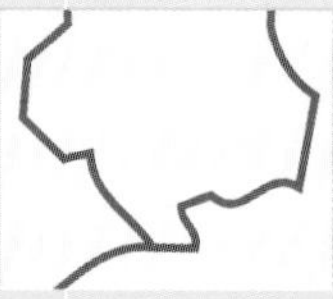

A gray line shows a country border. When countries are arguing about a border or are not sure where the border is, the line is dotted.

This picture shows where people drill into the land and seabed for oil, which is used to power all kinds of machines.

A blue line shows a river. The name of the river is written alongside. Rivers can run through many countries.

Different kinds of animals live in different parts of the world. Look for animals that live in the sea, on land and in the air.

This picture shows where people mine for diamonds. People also mine coal, silver, jewels, gold, copper, tin and iron.

Different people live around the world. Look for people playing sports or enjoying a traditional dance.

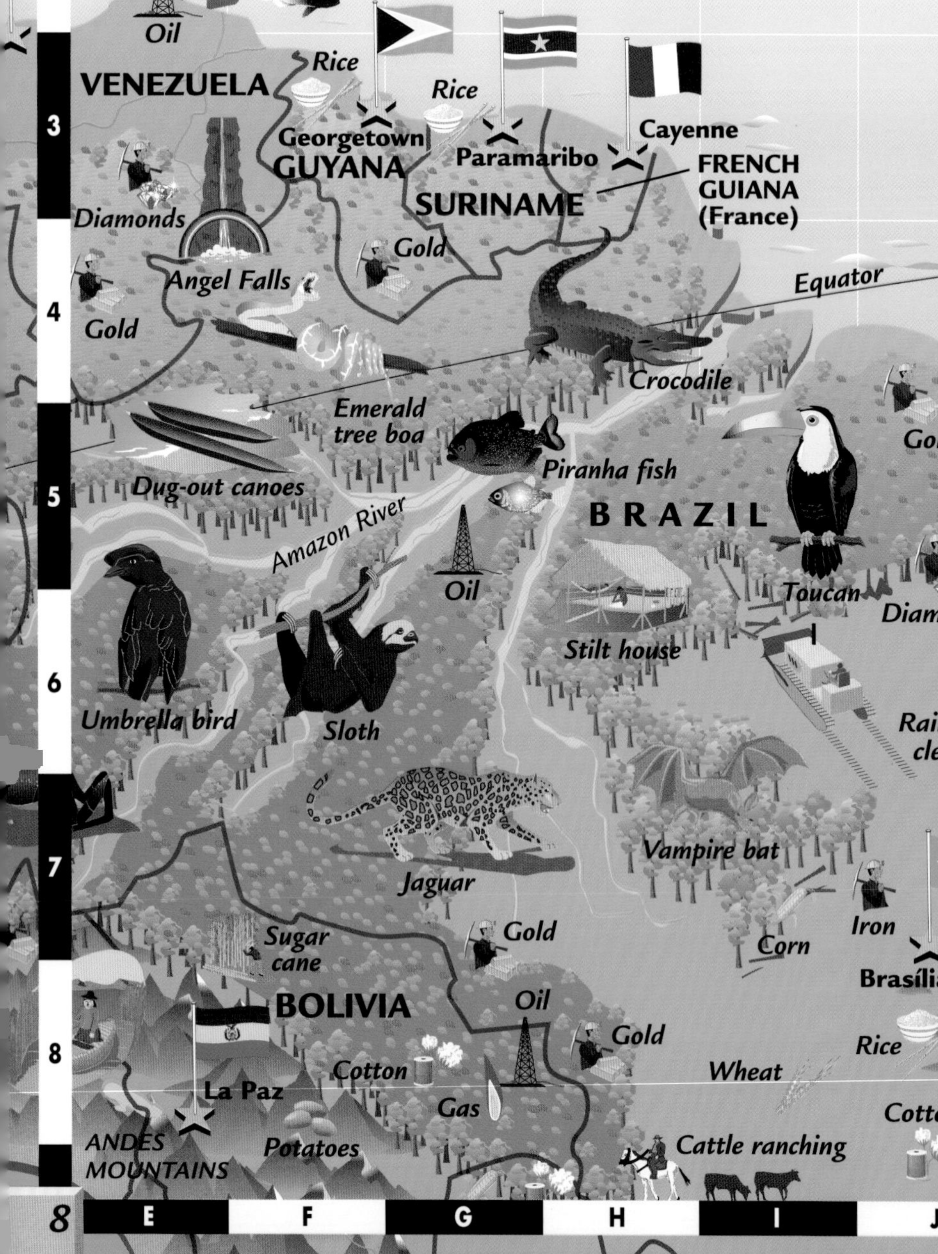

Oil

Royal gramma fish

VENEZUELA

Rice

Rice

Georgetown
GUYANA

Paramaribo
SURINAME

Cayenne
FRENCH GUIANA (France)

Diamonds

Gold

Angel Falls

Gold

Equator

Crocodile

Emerald tree boa

Piranha fish

Gold

Tobacco

Sugar cane

Cargo ships

Dug-out canoes

Amazon River

Oil

B R A Z I L

Cotton

Recife

Toucan

Diamonds

Stilt house

Gold

Umbrella bird

Sloth

Rainforest clearing

Oil

Shrimp

São Francisco River

Jaguar

Vampire bat

Cotton

Lobster

Gold

Iron

Corn

Sugar cane

BOLIVIA

Oil

Gold

Brasília

Rice

Oranges

Tourism

La Paz

Cotton

Gas

Wheat

Cotton

Iron

ANDES MOUNTAINS

Potatoes

Cattle ranching

Carnival

About the Factfile

Each map has a Factfile with facts about the places you can see. You might find out about a special animal or plant from a particular part of the world. Look at the picture beside each fact and then find it on the map. The facts in this Factfile are about the map of part of South America shown on the opposite page. Can you find all the pictures on the map?

On page 42, you will find a section of fascinating facts, full of many interesting things about the countries of the world.

Factfile

South America is home to nearly one quarter of all known animals and around 2,500 different kinds of trees.

The longest mountain range in the world is the Andes in South America.

Half of all the people in South America live in Brazil.

▼ This girl is answering the Fact Finder question. She is using a ruler and her finger to find the correct grid reference.

☞ FACT FINDER

Each map has a grid, which divides it into squares. The columns run up and down and have letters. The rows run from side to side and have numbers. This means each square has a name, or grid reference.

The Fact Finder asks questions about places on the map. You can find the answers by looking at the grid reference.

Here is a Fact Finder question about the map of part of South America shown on the opposite page.

▶ What is the name of the highest waterfall in the world? (See square E 4.)

To find square E 4, lay your ruler on column E, at the bottom of the map. Leave the ruler lying on the map. Now put your finger on row 4, at the side of the map. Run your finger along row 4 in a straight line. Square E 4 is where your finger meets the ruler.

You should have found Angel Falls which is in Venezuela.

World map

ALASKA (USA)

CANADA

UNITED STATES
OF AMERICA

GREENLAND
(Denmark)

These countries in Europe are shown more clearly inside the circle on page 11.

ARCTIC
OCEAN

FINLAND

NORW

ICELAND

THE
NETHERLANDS

SWEDEN

ESTONIA

LATVIA

UNITED
KINGDOM

REPUBLIC
OF IRELAND

BELGIUM

ANDORRA

FRANCE

PORTUGAL

SPAIN

ATLANTIC
OCEAN

BERMUDA (UK)

DOMINICAN REPUBLIC
PUERTO RICO (USA)
VIRGIN ISLANDS (USA & UK)
ANGUILLA (UK)
ST. KITTS & NEVIS
ANTIGUA & BARBUDA
GUADELOUPE (France)
DOMINICA
MARTINIQUE (France)
ST. LUCIA
BARBADOS
GRENADA
TRINIDAD & TOBAGO

MEXICO

BELIZE

BAHAMAS

CUBA

JAMAICA

HONDURAS HAITI

MONTSERRAT (UK)

GUATEMALA

EL SALVADOR

NICARAGUA

ST. VINCENT &
THE GRENADINES

COSTA RICA

PANAMA

VENEZUELA

GUYANA

SURINAME

FRENCH
GUIANA
(France)

GALAPAGOS
ISLANDS
(Ecuador)

COLOMBIA

ECUADOR

PERU

BRAZIL

PACIFIC
OCEAN

BOLIVIA

PARAGUAY

CHILE

URUGUAY

ARGENTINA

FALKLAND
ISLANDS
(UK)

SOUTH
GEORGIA
(UK)

AZORES
(Portugal)

MADEIRA
(Portugal)

CANARY
ISLANDS
(Spain)

BALEARIC
ISLANDS
(Spain)

MALTA

TUNISIA

CRE
(Gre

MOROCCO

ALGERIA

LIBYA

WESTERN
SAHARA

CAPE
VERDE
ISLANDS

MAURITANIA

MALI

NIGER

CHAD

GAMBIA

SENEGAL

GUINEA-
BISSAU

GUINEA

BURKINA
FASO

NIGERIA

CENTRA
AFRICA
REPUBL

SIERRA
LEONE

IVORY
COAST

GHANA

BENIN

TOGO

CAMEROON

LIBERIA

SÃO TOMÉ & PRÍNCIPE

GABON

DEMOCR
REPUBL
OF CON

EQUATORIAL
GUINEA

CONGO

CABINDA
(Angola)

ANGOLA

ZAM

NAMIBIA

BOTSWANA

ATLANTIC
OCEAN

REPUBLIC OF
SOUTH AFRICA

LESOTHO

ANTARCTICA

The world is divided into almost 200 countries and this map shows most of them. The countries are different colors so that you can tell them apart. Some countries own places in other parts of the world. In this atlas, these kinds of places have two labels. One label gives their name and another label in brackets gives the name of the country that owns them.

Some countries in Europe are crowded together. In this circle, we have made these countries bigger so that you can see them more easily.

The Arctic

The Arctic is the part of the world that lies closest to the North Pole. Around the Pole, the Arctic Ocean is frozen all year, but further away the ice and snow melt in the summer. In winter, the sun hardly shines which makes the Arctic very cold. Very little grows there, except for a few small plants such as moss or lichen.

FACT FINDER

► Which Arctic animal weighs more than nine grown men and lives on the moving ice? (See square F 8.)

► Which bird travels further than any other bird in the world? Every year it flies over 8,100 miles (13,000km) from the North to the South Pole? (See square F 7.)

► What do Arctic peoples often use to travel across the ice? (See E 8.)

ALASKA (USA)
CANADA
Inuit people
Snow goose
Moose
Coal
Lemming
Killer whales
Snowy owl
Arctic Circle
Arctic foxes
Oil
VICTORIA ISLAND (Canada)
Beluga whale
Hudson Bay
Arctic hare
North Pole expedition
Arctic tern
Lead
BAFFIN ISLAND (Canada)
ELLESMERE ISLAND (Canada)
Tents of the Sami people
Ice breakers
Snowmobile
RUSSIA
Walrus
Baffin Bay
North Pole ●
Polar bear
Ermine
Narwhal
Musk ox
ARCTIC OCEAN
GREENLAND (Denmark)
Hooded seal
Reindeer herding
Humpback whale
Ringed seals
Coal
ATLANTIC OCEAN
Guillemot
SVALBARD ISLANDS (Norway)
Puffins
Iron
ICELAND
Cod
Arctic Circle
S
SWEDEN
NORWAY

This distance is the same as 1,200 miles (1,900km) on the ground.

Factfile

The largest group of people in the Arctic are the Inuit. They have lived there for thousands of years.

The first person to travel to the North Pole from outside the Arctic was the American explorer, Robert Peary, in 1909.

The edge of the Arctic Ocean is one of the world's richest areas for fishing.

Antarctica

Antarctica is an enormous ice-covered continent near the South Pole. It is the coldest and windiest place on Earth. Few animals live around the pole but there are seals and birds on the coast, and plants and fish in the sea. The only people living in Antarctica are scientists. They stay on research stations to study the land and its wildlife.

Factfile

In 1911, Roald Amundsen, a Norwegian explorer, became the first person to reach the South Pole.

Up to 30,000 tourists a year cruise the waters around Antarctica to see the land and its wildlife.

Antarctica has many icebergs. The largest one ever found was three times the size of the island of Cyprus.

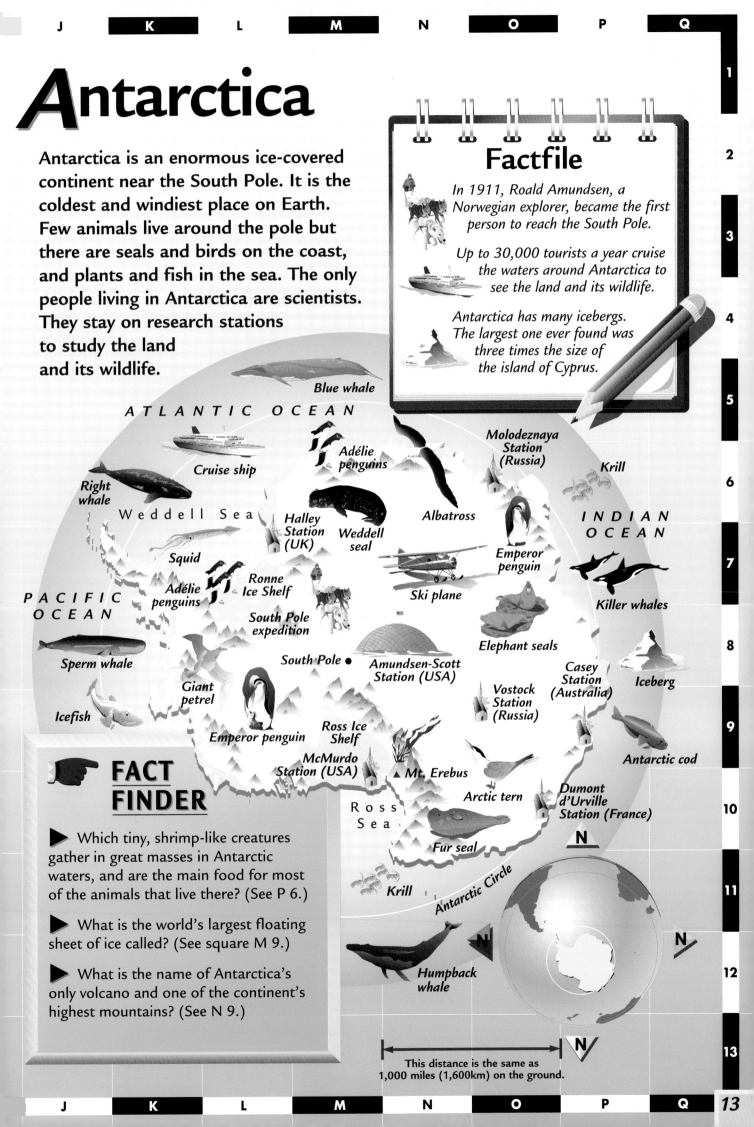

ATLANTIC OCEAN

Blue whale

Cruise ship

Right whale

Weddell Sea

Adélie penguins

Molodeznaya Station (Russia)

Krill

Halley Station (UK)

Albatross

INDIAN OCEAN

Weddell seal

Squid

Emperor penguin

Adélie penguins

Ronne Ice Shelf

Ski plane

Killer whales

PACIFIC OCEAN

South Pole expedition

Elephant seals

Sperm whale

South Pole ●

Amundsen-Scott Station (USA)

Casey Station (Australia)

Iceberg

Giant petrel

Vostock Station (Russia)

Emperor penguin

Ross Ice Shelf

McMurdo Station (USA)

▲ Mt. Erebus

Arctic tern

Dumont d'Urville Station (France)

Antarctic cod

Ross Sea

Fur seal

Krill

N

Antarctic Circle

Humpback whale

N

N

N

This distance is the same as 1,000 miles (1,600km) on the ground.

FACT FINDER

▶ Which tiny, shrimp-like creatures gather in great masses in Antarctic waters, and are the main food for most of the animals that live there? (See P 6.)

▶ What is the world's largest floating sheet of ice called? (See square M 9.)

▶ What is the name of Antarctica's only volcano and one of the continent's highest mountains? (See N 9.)

Canada

Canada is the second biggest country in the world after Russia. Large parts of it are cold and empty. In the north, there are huge pine forests and the weather is often freezing. Most people live in the south where it is warmer. Canada produces oil and mines coal, silver, gold and copper. It has good farmland, where farmers grow enormous fields of wheat. It also has large factories, mostly in the east, that make and sell goods, such as cars, trucks and trains.

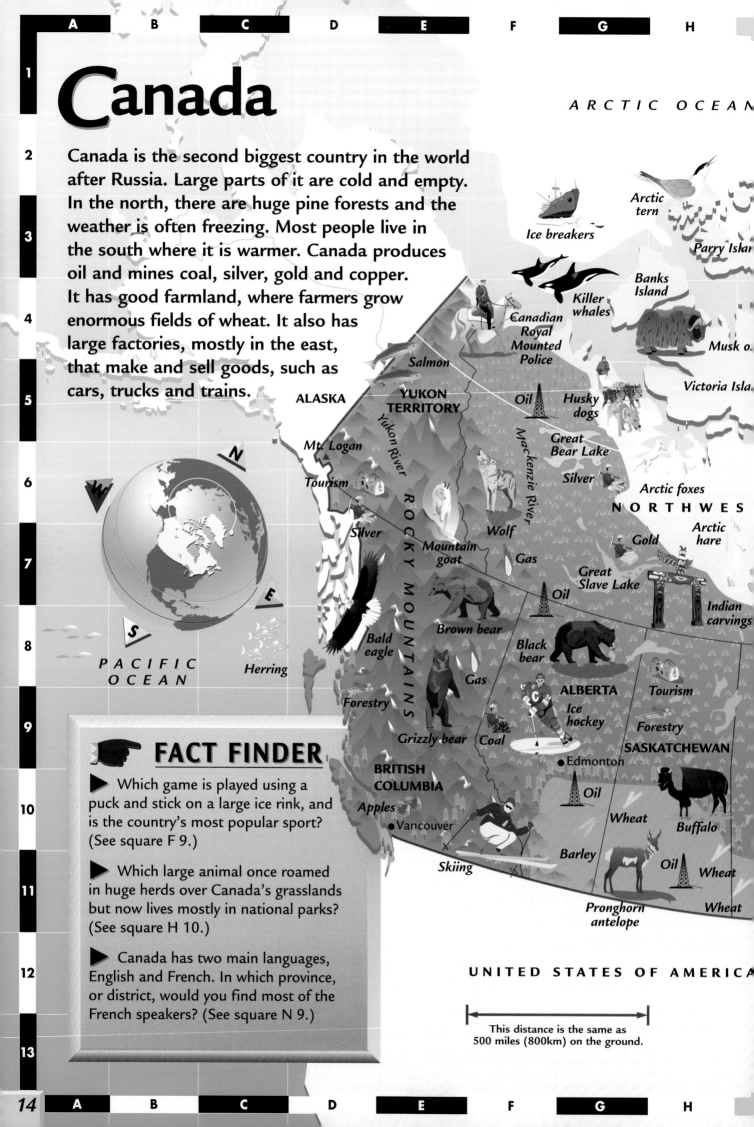

ARCTIC OCEAN

Ice breakers

Arctic tern

Parry Island

Banks Island

Killer whales

Canadian Royal Mounted Police

Musk o.

Victoria Isla.

Salmon

YUKON TERRITORY

Oil

Husky dogs

ALASKA

Mt. Logan

Yukon River

Great Bear Lake

Silver

Arctic foxes

NORTHWES

Tourism

Mackenzie River

Silver

ROCKY MOUNTAINS

Mountain goat

Wolf

Gas

Gold

Arctic hare

Great Slave Lake

Oil

Indian carvings

Brown bear

Black bear

Bald eagle

N
W
E
S

PACIFIC OCEAN

Herring

Grizzly bear

Gas

Coal

Forestry

Ice hockey

ALBERTA

Tourism

Forestry

SASKATCHEWAN

BRITISH COLUMBIA

Edmonton

Apples

Vancouver

Oil

Wheat

Buffalo

Skiing

Barley

Oil

Wheat

Pronghorn antelope

Wheat

FACT FINDER

▶ Which game is played using a puck and stick on a large ice rink, and is the country's most popular sport? (See square F 9.)

▶ Which large animal once roamed in huge herds over Canada's grasslands but now lives mostly in national parks? (See square H 10.)

▶ Canada has two main languages, English and French. In which province, or district, would you find most of the French speakers? (See square N 9.)

UNITED STATES OF AMERICA

This distance is the same as 500 miles (800km) on the ground.

Ellesmere
Island

GREENLAND
(Denmark)

Queen
Elizabeth Islands   Lemming

Walrus

Beluga whale

Hooded seal

Narwhal

Prince
of Wales
Island

Inuit
people

Baffin Island

Snowy
owl

Snowmobile

Arctic Circle

Polar bear

ERRITORIES

Starfish

Humpback whale

ATLANTIC
OCEAN

Canada geese

Ice breakers

Lynx

Iron

Puffins

Right whale

Moose

Hudson
Bay

Mink

Snow goose

Float plane

NEWFOUNDLAND

Cod

ANITOBA

Nelson River

QUEBEC

Iron

Forestry

pper   Beaver

Ermine

Forestry

Maple
syrup

Making
paper

Gulf
of
St. Lawrence

Tourism

ONTARIO

Gray squirrel

Gold

Tourist bus

Copper

Dairy
cattle

Oil

Road train

Château
Frontenac

NEW
BRUNSWICK

NOVA SCOTIA

Winnipeg

Raccoon

Iron

Potatoes

Apples

ef cattle   Iron

Lake Superior

CN Tower

Montreal

Coal

PRINCE
EDWARD
ISLAND

Blue whale

Lake
Huron

Ottawa

Car building

Toronto   Lake Ontario

Lake
Michigan

Pigs

Lobster

Lake Erie   Niagara Falls

Factfile

Pine forests cover more than
one-third of Canada. The trees
are cut down by lumberjacks and
made into timber and paper.

Canada is famous for its sweet
maple syrup. It is made in the
spring from the sticky sap of
sugar maple trees.

In Canada no one is far from water.
The country has over one million
lakes. Lake Superior, on the
border between Canada and
the United States, is the
largest freshwater lake
in the world.

St. Lawrence River

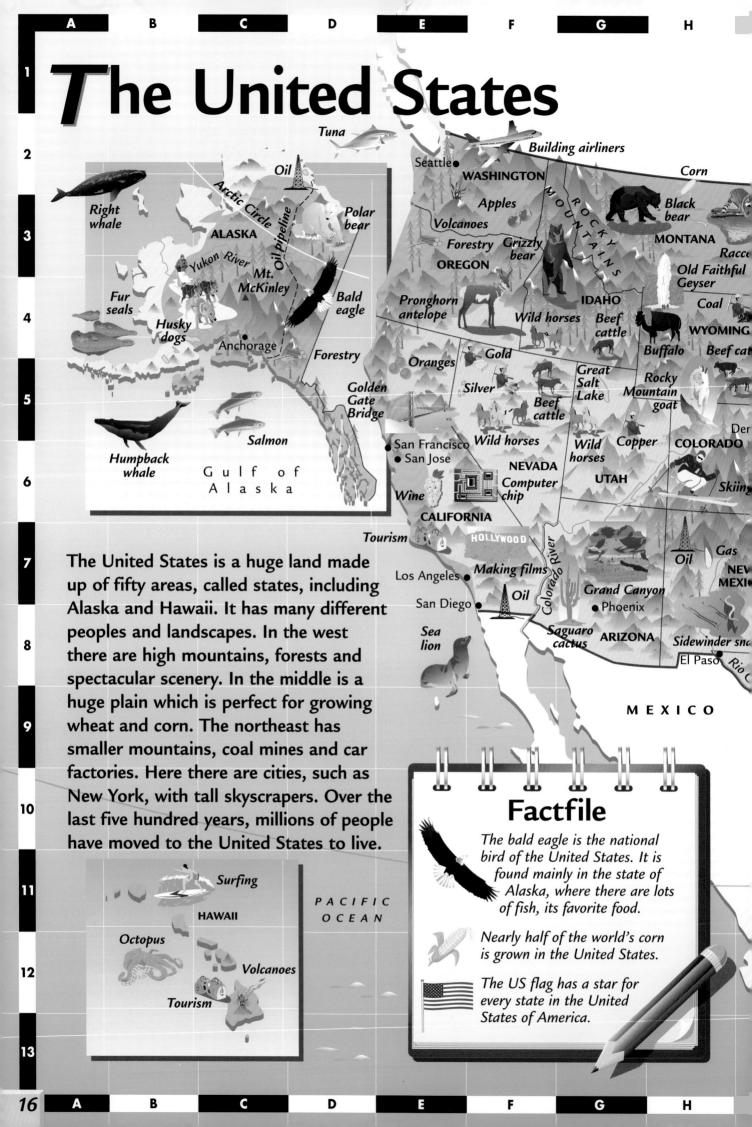

The United States

Tuna

Building airliners

Corn

Seattle●

WASHINGTON

Apples

Black bear

Oil

Volcanoes

Forestry

Grizzly bear

MONTANA

Racce...

Right whale

ALASKA

Polar bear

Arctic Circle

Oil pipeline

OREGON

Old Faithful Geyser

Coal

Yukon River

Mt. McKinley

Bald eagle

Pronghorn antelope

Wild horses

IDAHO

Beef cattle

WYOMING

Fur seals

Husky dogs

Anchorage●

Forestry

Oranges

Gold

Great Salt Lake

Buffalo

Beef cat...

Golden Gate Bridge

Silver

Beef cattle

Rocky Mountain goat

Copper

COLORADO

Der...

Humpback whale

Salmon

San Francisco●
●San Jose

Wild horses

Wild horses

Gulf of Alaska

Wine

NEVADA
Computer chip

UTAH

Skiing

CALIFORNIA

HOLLYWOOD

Colorado River

Oil

Gas

Tourism

Making films

Grand Canyon

NEW MEXI...

Los Angeles●

Oil

Phoenix●

Saguaro cactus

ARIZONA

Sidewinder sna...

San Diego●

Sea lion

El Paso●

Rio G...

MEXICO

The United States is a huge land made up of fifty areas, called states, including Alaska and Hawaii. It has many different peoples and landscapes. In the west there are high mountains, forests and spectacular scenery. In the middle is a huge plain which is perfect for growing wheat and corn. The northeast has smaller mountains, coal mines and car factories. Here there are cities, such as New York, with tall skyscrapers. Over the last five hundred years, millions of people have moved to the United States to live.

Surfing

HAWAII

PACIFIC OCEAN

Octopus

Volcanoes

Tourism

Factfile

The bald eagle is the national bird of the United States. It is found mainly in the state of Alaska, where there are lots of fish, its favorite food.

Nearly half of the world's corn is grown in the United States.

The US flag has a star for every state in the United States of America.

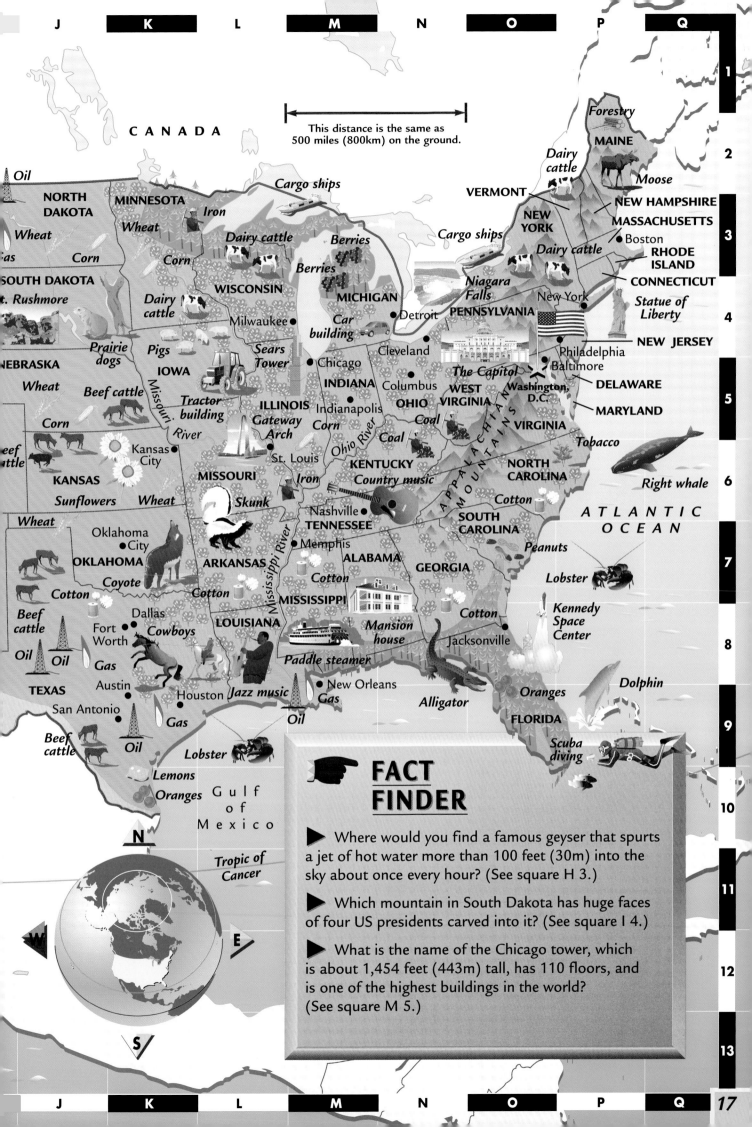

FACT FINDER

▶ Where would you find a famous geyser that spurts a jet of hot water more than 100 feet (30m) into the sky about once every hour? (See square H 3.)

▶ Which mountain in South Dakota has huge faces of four US presidents carved into it? (See square I 4.)

▶ What is the name of the Chicago tower, which is about 1,454 feet (443m) tall, has 110 floors, and is one of the highest buildings in the world? (See square M 5.)

Mexico, Central America and the Caribbean

UNITED STATES OF AMERICA

N
W
E
S

Saguaro cactus

BAJA CALIFORNIA

Beef cattle

Cotton

SIERRA

Silver

Sea lion

Rice

Coyote

MADRE

Beef cattle

Elephant seals

Blue whale

MEXICO

Rio Grande

Armadillo

Gulf of Mexico

Cotton

Lobster

Anchovies

P A C I F I C
O C E A N

Spectacled bear

Grapefruit

Lemons

Tobacco

Tourism

Corn

Oranges

Chichén Itzá

Tourism

Humpback whale

Corn

Forestry

Shrimp

Polka dot grouper fish

Iron

Oil

Scarlet macaw

Spider monkey

Tourism

Mexico City

Sugar cane

Acapulco

Corn   Corn

Belmopa[n]

BELIZE

Coffee

Factfile

Mexico is one of the world's biggest producers of silver.

The Caribbean Islands are some of the world's most popular holiday places. Cruise ships carry passengers from one island to another.

Honduras is one of the world's largest producers of bananas. The fruit is green when it is picked, but ripens as it is shipped across the world.

Teardrop butterfly fish

GUATEMALA

Guatemala City

San Salvador

Tegu[cigalp]a

EL SALVADOR

Coffee

Managua

Swordfish

Clown fish

This distance is the same as 430 miles (700km) on the ground.

Sea horses

Sperm whale

To the south of the United States, a narrow strip of land containing eight countries links North America with South America. The largest of these is Mexico, a country with a long history and contrasting landscapes. Further south are the seven nations of Central America. Many people in Central America are farmers, who grow food for themselves or work on sugar, coffee or banana plantations. Further east, in the warm Caribbean Sea, lie hundreds of sun-drenched islands. They are famous for their coral reefs and beautiful sandy beaches.

FACT FINDER

▶ In Central America, which ancient city was built by an American Indian people called the Maya over one thousand years ago? (See square H 8.)

▶ Which shortcut is used by cargo ships to sail between the Atlantic and Pacific Oceans. It is about 51 miles (82km) long and about 30 ships pass through it each day. (See square K 12.)

▶ Which is the only kind of bear to live in Central America? It is named after the white circles around its eyes. (See D 7.)

▶ Which is one of the largest cities in the world, where more people live than in the whole of Australia? (See square E 8.)

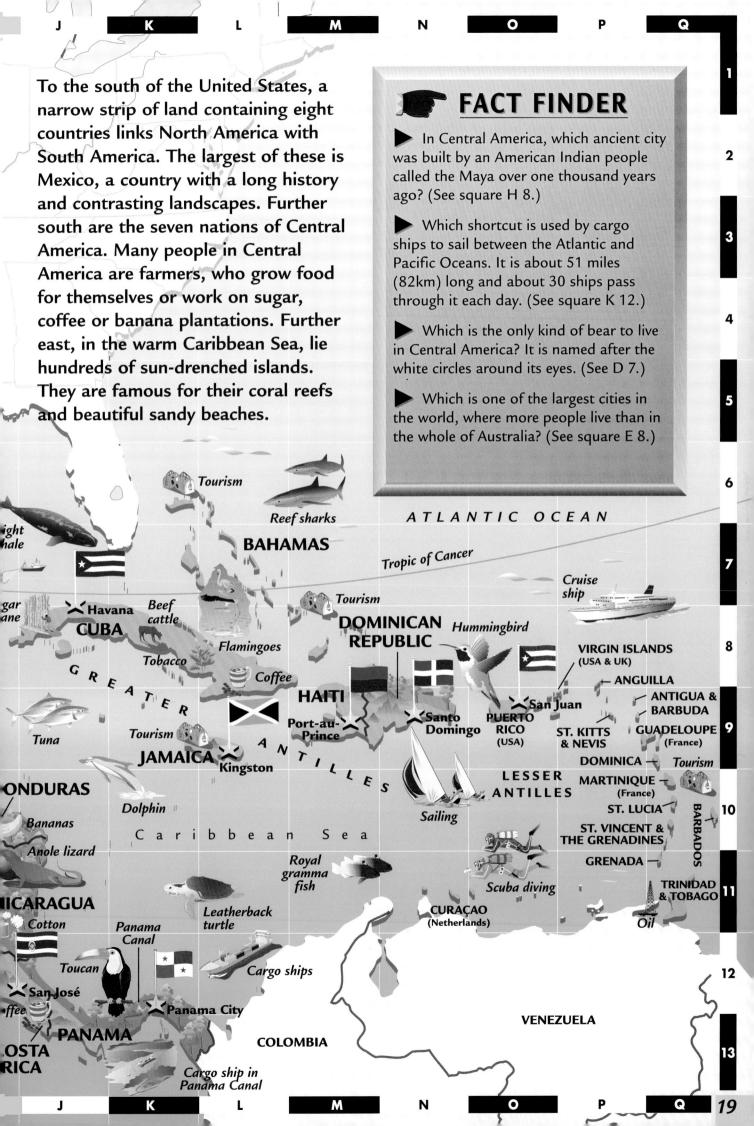

Tourism

Reef sharks

BAHAMAS

Tropic of Cancer

A T L A N T I C   O C E A N

Cruise ship

ight hale

gar ane

✈ **Havana**
CUBA

Beef cattle

Tourism

DOMINICAN REPUBLIC

Hummingbird

VIRGIN ISLANDS
(USA & UK)

Flamingoes

— **ANGUILLA**

Tobacco

Coffee

G R E A T E R

HAITI

San Juan

ANTIGUA & BARBUDA

Tuna

Port-au-Prince

Santo Domingo

PUERTO RICO
(USA)

ST. KITTS & NEVIS

GUADELOUPE
(France)

Tourism

A N T I L L E S

DOMINICA —

Tourism

JAMAICA ✈
Kingston

LESSER ANTILLES

MARTINIQUE —
(France)

ONDURAS

Dolphin

C a r i b b e a n   S e a

Sailing

ST. LUCIA —

BARBADOS

Bananas

Anole lizard

ST. VINCENT & THE GRENADINES

Royal gramma fish

GRENADA —

TRINIDAD & TOBAGO

ICARAGUA

Leatherback turtle

Scuba diving

Cotton

Panama Canal

CURAÇAO
(Netherlands)

Oil

Toucan

Cargo ships

✈ **San José**

✈ **Panama City**

VENEZUELA

ffee

PANAMA

COLOMBIA

OSTA RICA

Cargo ship in Panama Canal

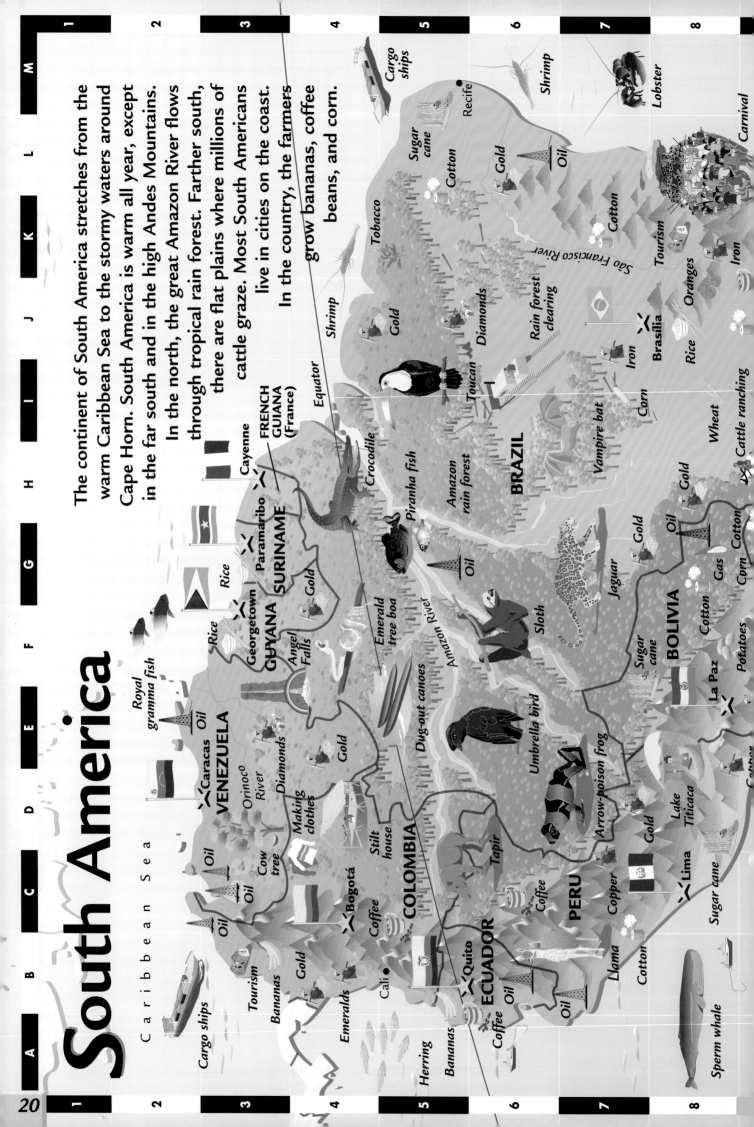

South America

The continent of South America stretches from the warm Caribbean Sea to the stormy waters around Cape Horn. South America is warm all year, except in the far south and in the high Andes Mountains. In the north, the great Amazon River flows through tropical rain forest. Farther south, there are flat plains where millions of cattle graze. Most South Americans live in cities on the coast. In the country, the farmers grow bananas, coffee beans, and corn.

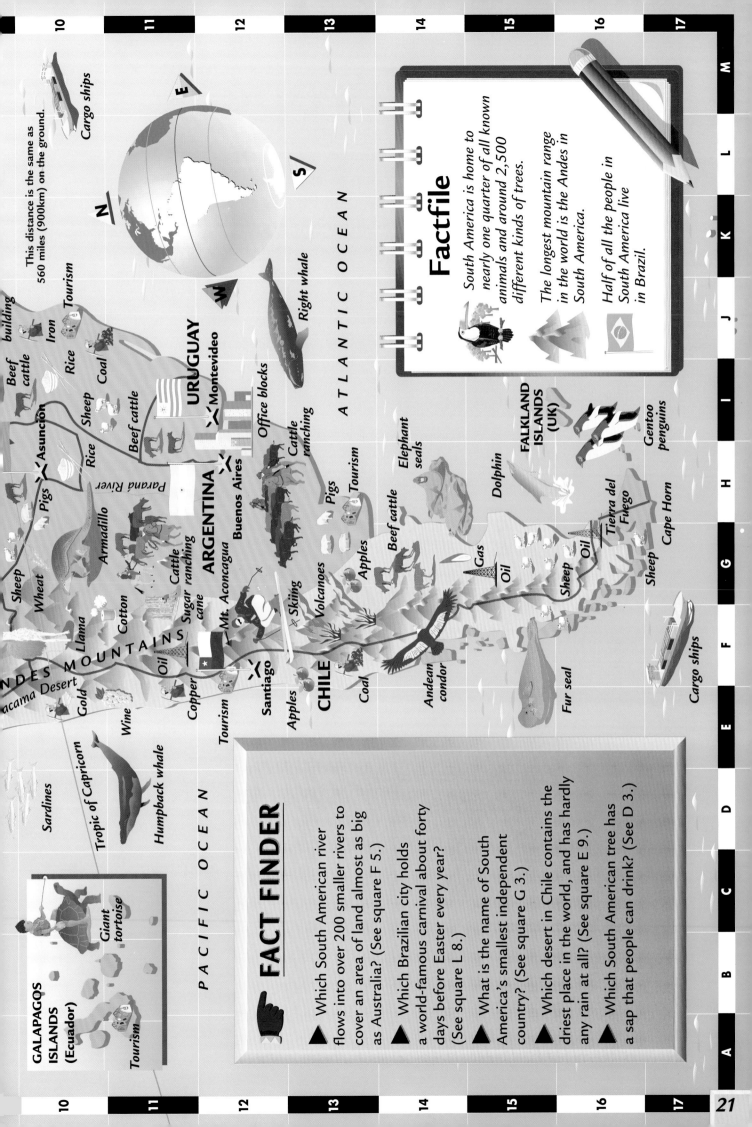

This distance is the same as 560 miles (900km) on the ground.

N | E | S | W

GALAPAGOS ISLANDS (Ecuador)
Giant tortoise
Tourism

PACIFIC OCEAN

Sardines
Humpback whale
Tropic of Capricorn

building
Beef cattle
Iron
Tourism
Rice
Coal
Sheep
Rice
Beef cattle
Asunción
Pigs
Rice
Paraná River

Sheep
Wheat
Llama
Cotton
Armadillo
Cattle
Sugar ranching
Oil
Gold
Copper
Wine
Atacama Desert
ANDES MOUNTAINS
Mt. Aconcagua
Tourism
Sugar cane
Cotton

ARGENTINA
Buenos Aires
Santiago
Apples
Skiing
Volcanoes
Apples
Coal
CHILE
Andean condor

URUGUAY
Montevideo
Office blocks
Cattle ranching
Pigs
Tourism
Beef cattle
Beef cattle
Elephant seals
Gas
Oil

Right whale

ATLANTIC OCEAN

Dolphin
Fur seal
Cargo ships

FALKLAND ISLANDS (UK)
Gentoo penguins
Sheep
Oil
Tierra del Fuego
Sheep
Cape Horn

Cargo ships

Factfile

South America is home to nearly one quarter of all known animals and around 2,500 different kinds of trees.

The longest mountain range in the world is the Andes in South America.

Half of all the people in South America live in Brazil.

☞ FACT FINDER

▲ Which South American river flows into over 200 smaller rivers to cover an area of land almost as big as Australia? (See square F 5.)

▲ Which Brazilian city holds a world-famous carnival about forty days before Easter every year? (See square L 8.)

▲ What is the name of South America's smallest independent country? (See square G 3.)

▲ Which desert in Chile contains the driest place in the world, and has hardly any rain at all? (See square E 9.)

▲ Which South American tree has a sap that people can drink? (See D 3.)

21

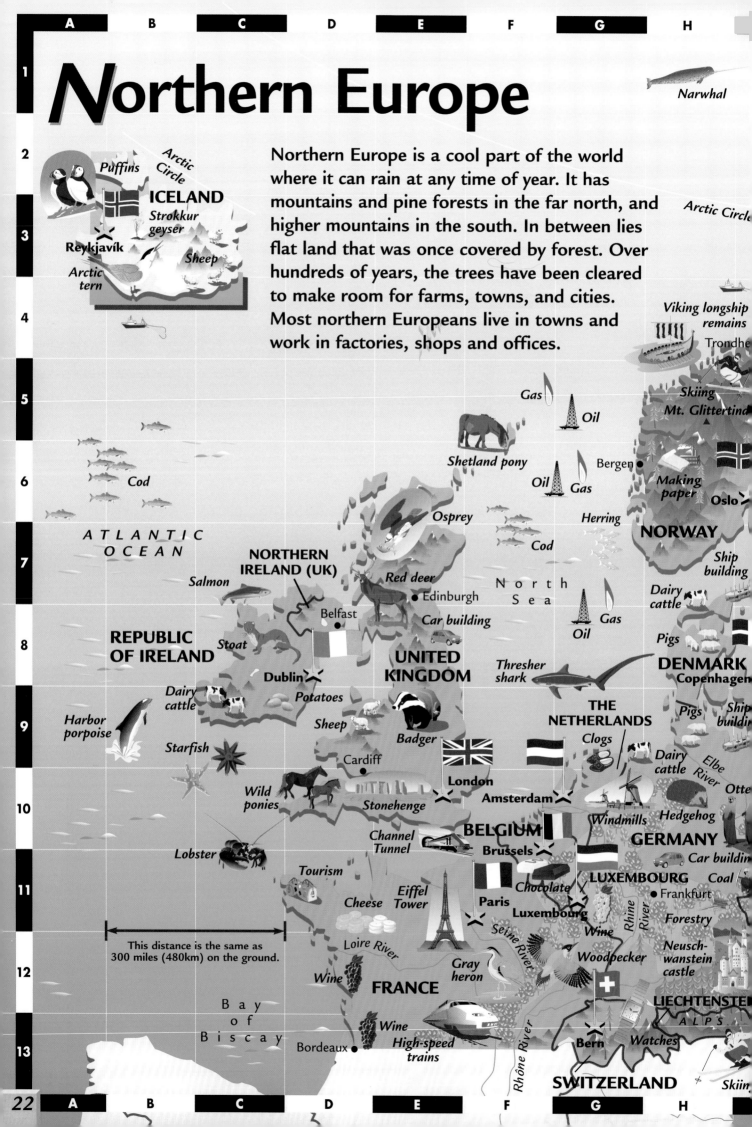

Northern Europe

Narwhal

Puffins

Arctic Circle

ICELAND

Strokkur geyser

Reykjavík

Arctic tern

Sheep

Northern Europe is a cool part of the world where it can rain at any time of year. It has mountains and pine forests in the far north, and higher mountains in the south. In between lies flat land that was once covered by forest. Over hundreds of years, the trees have been cleared to make room for farms, towns, and cities. Most northern Europeans live in towns and work in factories, shops and offices.

Arctic Circle

Viking longship remains

Trondhe

Skiing

Mt. Glittertind

Gas

Oil

Shetland pony

Bergen

Making paper

Oslo

Oil *Gas*

Osprey

Herring

NORWAY

Cod

Ship building

A T L A N T I C
O C E A N

Cod

NORTHERN IRELAND (UK)

Red deer

N o r t h
S e a

Dairy cattle

Salmon

Edinburgh

Belfast

Car building

Oil

Gas

Pigs

REPUBLIC OF IRELAND

Stoat

UNITED KINGDOM

Thresher shark

DENMARK

Copenhagen

Harbor porpoise

Dairy cattle

Dublin

Potatoes

Sheep

Badger

THE NETHERLANDS

Clogs

Pigs

Ship buildi

Starfish

Cardiff

London

Dairy cattle

Elbe River

Wild ponies

Stonehenge

Amsterdam

Windmills

Hedgehog

Lobster

Channel Tunnel

BELGIUM

GERMANY

Brussels

Car buildin

LUXEMBOURG

Coal

Tourism

Chotolate

Frankfurt

Cheese

Eiffel Tower

Paris

Luxembourg

Rhine River

Forestry

This distance is the same as 300 miles (480km) on the ground.

Wine

Woodpecker

Neuschwanstein castle

Loire River

Gray heron

Seine River

Wine

Wine

FRANCE

LIECHTENSTEI

B a y
o f
B i s c a y

A L P S

Wine

Bern

Watches

Bordeaux

High-speed trains

Rhône River

Skiin

SWITZERLAND

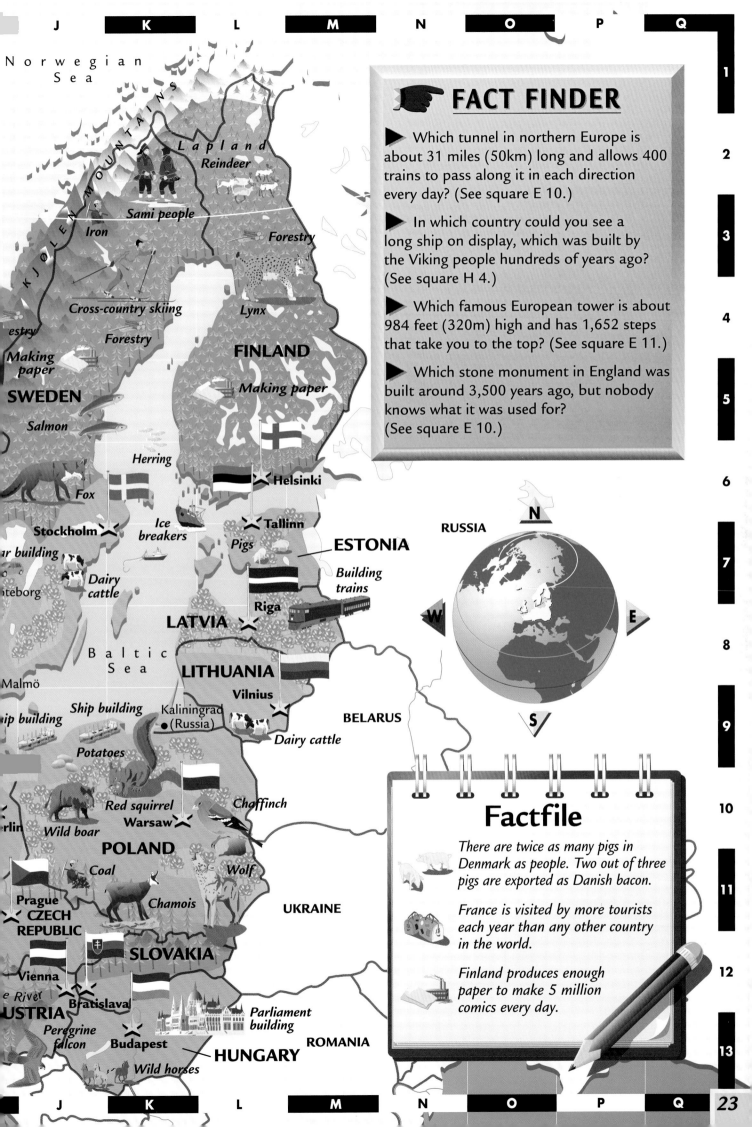

Top/side grid letters: J K L M N O P Q
Side numbers: 1 2 3 4 5 6 7 8 9 10 11 12 13

Norwegian Sea

Kjølen Mountains

Lapland

Reindeer

Sami people

Iron

Forestry

Cross-country skiing

Forestry

Lynx

FINLAND

Making paper

Making paper

SWEDEN

Salmon

Herring

Helsinki

Fox

Ice breakers

Tallinn

Stockholm

Pigs

ESTONIA

Building trains

Dairy cattle

Riga

LATVIA

Baltic Sea

Göteborg

Malmö

LITHUANIA

Ship building

Vilnius

Kaliningrad (Russia)

Dairy cattle

BELARUS

Potatoes

Red squirrel

Chaffinch

Wild boar

Warsaw

POLAND

Coal

Wolf

Prague

CZECH REPUBLIC

Chamois

UKRAINE

SLOVAKIA

Vienna

e River

Bratislava

AUSTRIA

Peregrine falcon

Budapest

Parliament building

ROMANIA

HUNGARY

Wild horses

FACT FINDER

▶ Which tunnel in northern Europe is about 31 miles (50km) long and allows 400 trains to pass along it in each direction every day? (See square E 10.)

▶ In which country could you see a long ship on display, which was built by the Viking people hundreds of years ago? (See square H 4.)

▶ Which famous European tower is about 984 feet (320m) high and has 1,652 steps that take you to the top? (See square E 11.)

▶ Which stone monument in England was built around 3,500 years ago, but nobody knows what it was used for? (See square E 10.)

RUSSIA

N
W
E
S

Factfile

There are twice as many pigs in Denmark as people. Two out of three pigs are exported as Danish bacon.

France is visited by more tourists each year than any other country in the world.

Finland produces enough paper to make 5 million comics every day.

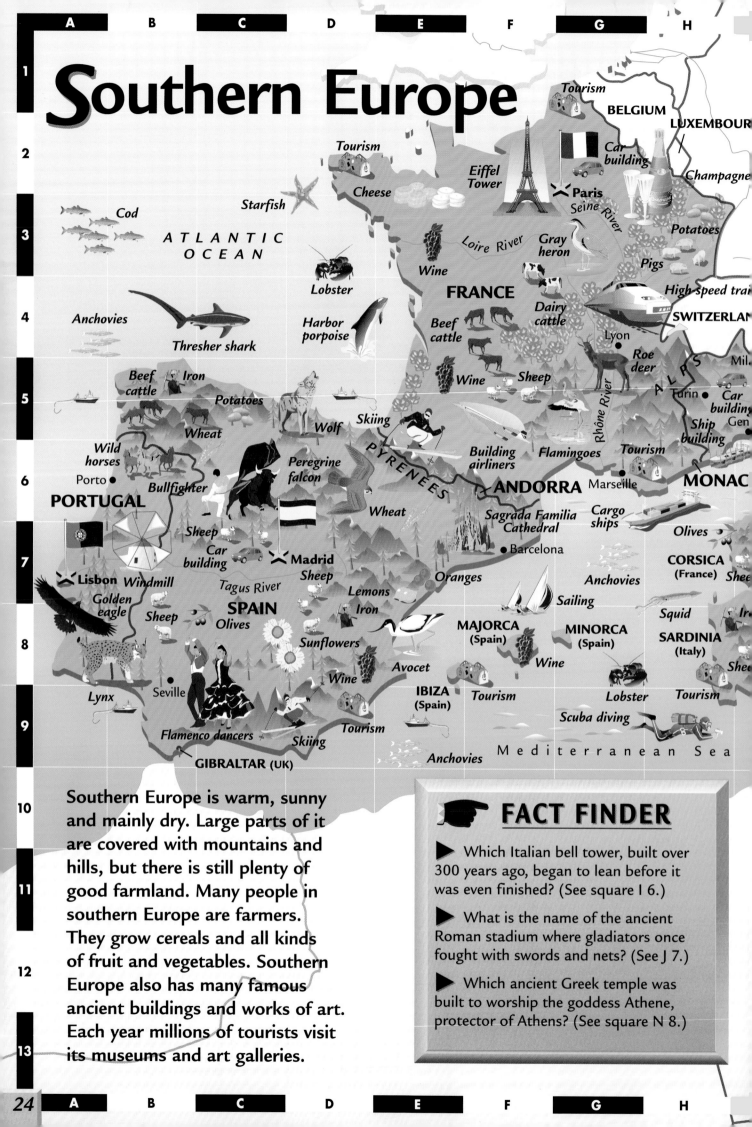

Southern Europe

BELGIUM

LUXEMBOUR

Tourism

Eiffel Tower

Car building

Champagne

Tourism

Cheese

Paris

Seine River

Potatoes

Cod

Starfish

A T L A N T I C
O C E A N

Wine

Loire River

Gray heron

Pigs

FRANCE

High speed trai

Lobster

Dairy cattle

SWITZERLAN

Anchovies

Harbor porpoise

Beef cattle

Lyon

Roe deer

Mil.

Thresher shark

Wine

Sheep

Turin

A L P S

Car building

Beef cattle

Iron

Gen

Potatoes

Skiing

Rhône River

Ship building

Wild horses

Wheat

Wolf

Building airliners

Flamingoes

Tourism

Porto

Bullfighter

Peregrine falcon

P Y R E N E E S

ANDORRA

Marseille

MONAC

PORTUGAL

Cargo ships

Olives

Sheep

Wheat

Sagrada Familia Cathedral

CORSICA
(France)

She

Lisbon

Car building

Madrid

Barcelona

Anchovies

Golden eagle

Windmill

Sheep

Tagus River

Oranges

Sailing

Squid

Lemons

SPAIN

Sheep

Ir

Olives

Iron

MAJORCA
(Spain)

MINORCA
(Spain)

SARDINIA
(Italy)

Lynx

Sunflowers

Avocet

Wine

She

Seville

Flamenco dancers

Wine

IBIZA
(Spain)

Tourism

Lobster

Tourism

Scuba diving

Skiing

Tourism

GIBRALTAR (UK)

Anchovies

M e d i t e r r a n e a n   S e a

Southern Europe is warm, sunny
and mainly dry. Large parts of it
are covered with mountains and
hills, but there is still plenty of
good farmland. Many people in
southern Europe are farmers.
They grow cereals and all kinds
of fruit and vegetables. Southern
Europe also has many famous
ancient buildings and works of art.
Each year millions of tourists visit
its museums and art galleries.

👉 FACT FINDER

▶ Which Italian bell tower, built over
300 years ago, began to lean before it
was even finished? (See square I 6.)

▶ What is the name of the ancient
Roman stadium where gladiators once
fought with swords and nets? (See J 7.)

▶ Which ancient Greek temple was
built to worship the goddess Athene,
protector of Athens? (See square N 8.)

Factfile

Mount Etna in Sicily is the largest volcano in Europe. It last erupted in 1995.

Spain produces more olive oil than any other country. Each year it produces enough olive oil to fill 160 Olympic-sized swimming pools.

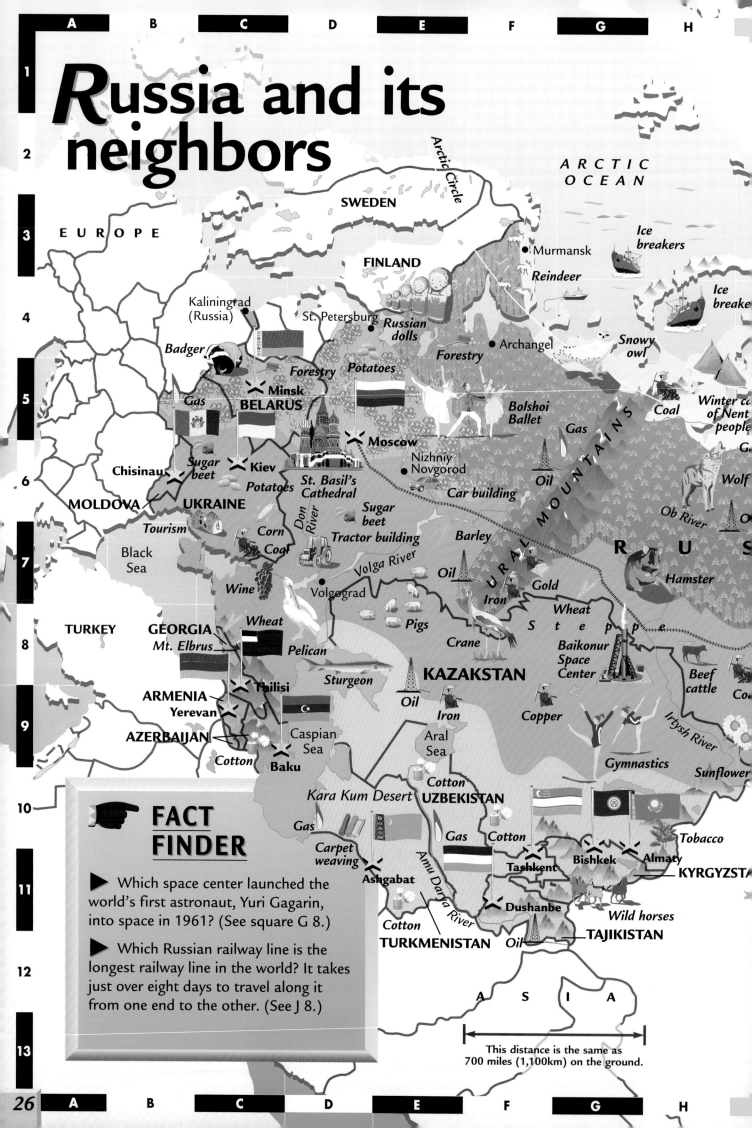

Russia and its neighbors

A B C D E F G H

1 2 3 4 5 6 7 8 9 10 11 12 13

SWEDEN

Arctic Circle

ARCTIC OCEAN

EUROPE

FINLAND

Ice breakers

Murmansk

Reindeer

Ice breake

Kaliningrad (Russia)

St. Petersburg

Russian dolls

Archangel

Forestry

Snowy owl

Winter ca of Nent people

Badger

Forestry

Potatoes

Gas

Minsk

BELARUS

Moscow

Bolshoi Ballet

Coal

G

Chisinau

Sugar beet

Kiev

St. Basil's Cathedral

Nizhniy Novgorod

Gas

Wolf

MOLDOVA

Potatoes

UKRAINE

Don River

Sugar beet

Car building

Oil

Ob River

Tourism

Corn

Coal

Tractor building

Barley

Gold

Hamster

R U S

Black Sea

Wine

Volga River

Oil

Wheat

Step e

TURKEY

Wheat

Volgograd

Iron

Pigs

Crane

Baikonur Space Center

Beef cattle

Co

GEORGIA

Mt. Elbrus

Pelican

KAZAKSTAN

ARMENIA

Tbilisi

Sturgeon

Copper

Irtysh River

Yerevan

Oil

Iron

Gymnastics

Sunflower

AZERBAIJAN

Caspian Sea

Aral Sea

Cotton

Baku

Cotton

Tobacco

Cotton

Kara Kum Desert

UZBEKISTAN

Gas

Gas

Cotton

Bishkek

Almaty

KYRGYZSTA

Carpet weaving

Tashkent

Dushanbe

Wild horses

Ashgabat

Amu Darya River

Cotton

Oil

TAJIKISTAN

TURKMENISTAN

A S I A

FACT FINDER

► Which space center launched the world's first astronaut, Yuri Gagarin, into space in 1961? (See square G 8.)

► Which Russian railway line is the longest railway line in the world? It takes just over eight days to travel along it from one end to the other. (See J 8.)

This distance is the same as 700 miles (1,100km) on the ground.

A B C D E F G H

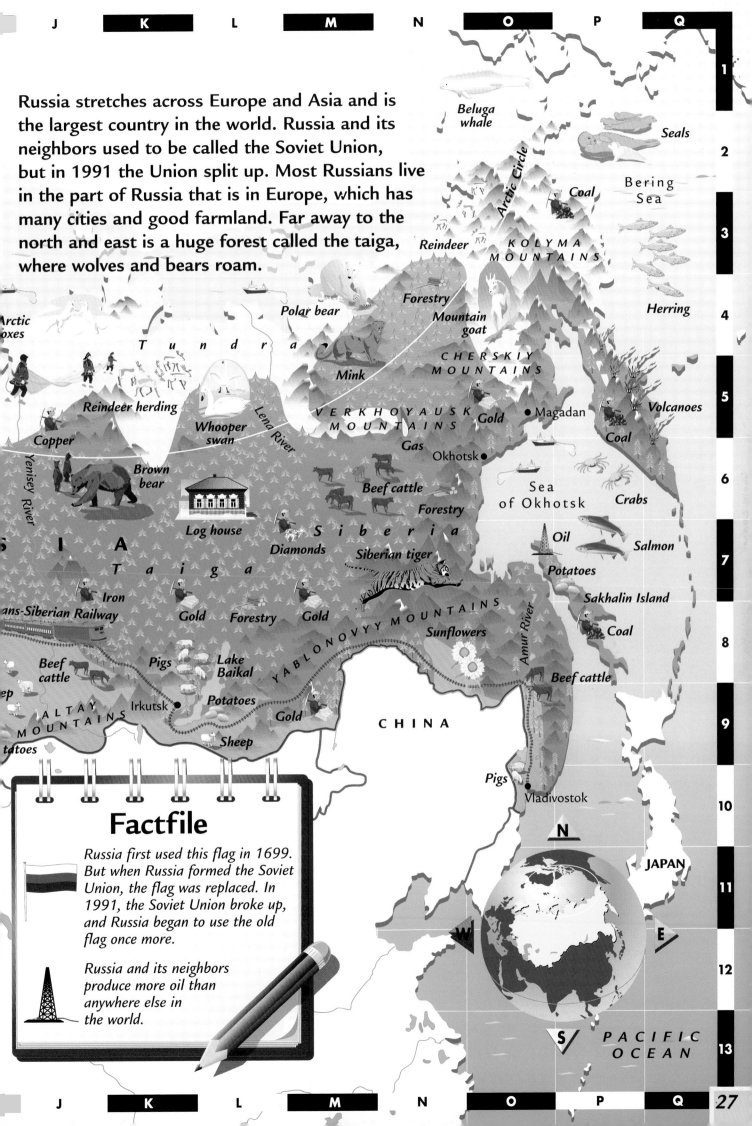

Russia stretches across Europe and Asia and is the largest country in the world. Russia and its neighbors used to be called the Soviet Union, but in 1991 the Union split up. Most Russians live in the part of Russia that is in Europe, which has many cities and good farmland. Far away to the north and east is a huge forest called the taiga, where wolves and bears roam.

Factfile

Russia first used this flag in 1699. But when Russia formed the Soviet Union, the flag was replaced. In 1991, the Soviet Union broke up, and Russia began to use the old flag once more.

Russia and its neighbors produce more oil than anywhere else in the world.

The Middle East

The southwest corner of Asia is also called the Middle East. Here, thousands of years ago, people first became farmers, then settled close together in towns. Much of the land in southwest Asia is hot, dry desert, which can be hard to farm. Fifty years ago, people found oil under the desert. They used the money they made from the oil to build huge watering systems, so they could grow crops more easily in the poor soil. They also built large cities.

Factfile

Over 5,000 years ago, the first cities in the world grew up in southwest Asia, along the Tigris and Euphrates Rivers.

Three of the world's major religions began in southwest Asia. They are Islam, Judaism and Christianity.

The Middle East makes some of the world's most expensive hand-made carpets. Carpet-makers weave and knot wool to make different patterns which can tell you the area the carpet comes from.

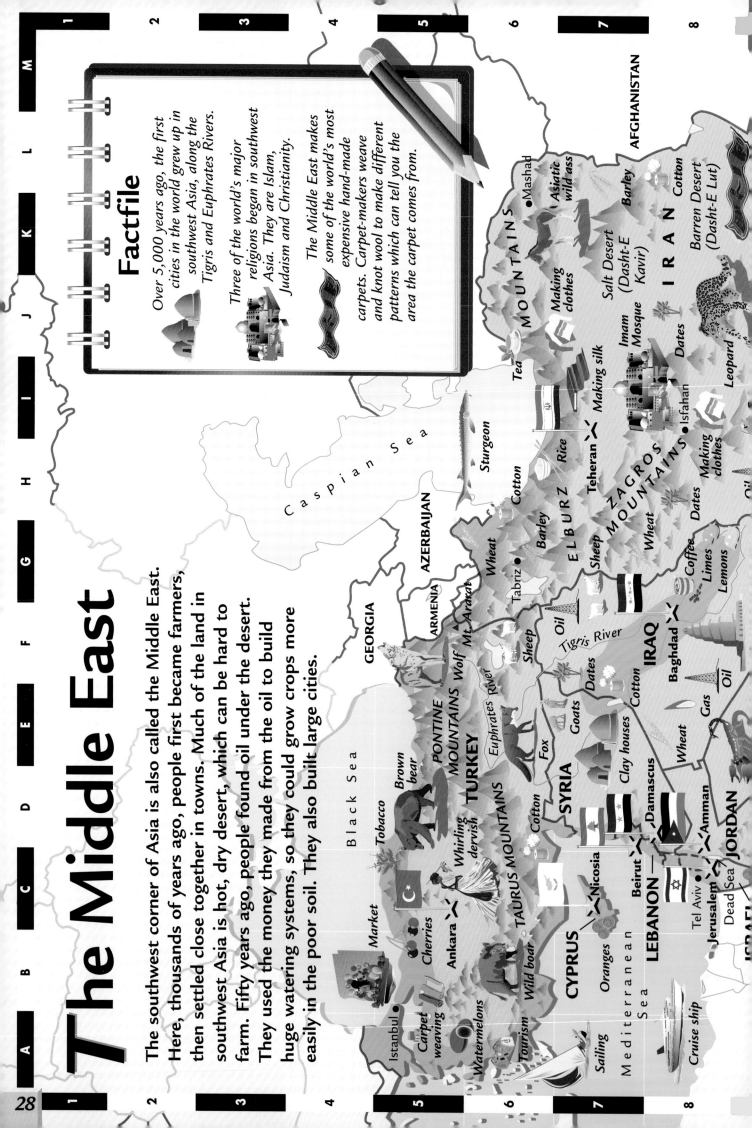

Black Sea

Mediterranean Sea

Caspian Sea

Market

Tobacco

Brown bear

Cherries

Ankara

Whirling dervish

PONTINE MOUNTAINS

Wolf

Mt Ararat

Euphrates River

TAURUS MOUNTAINS

TURKEY

Istanbul

Carpet weaving

Watermelons

Tourism

Wild boar

Sailing

Oranges

CYPRUS

Nicosia

Cotton

SYRIA

Damascus

Clay houses

Goats

Fox

Dates

Oil

Tigris River

Sheep

Wheat

Cotton

Gas

Oil

Baghdad

IRAQ

Wheat

LEBANON

Beirut

Tel Aviv

Jerusalem

Dead Sea

Amman

JORDAN

ISRAEL

Cruise ship

GEORGIA

ARMENIA

AZERBAIJAN

Sturgeon

Cotton

Wheat

Barley

Tabriz

Sheep

Rice

Teheran

ELBURZ MOUNTAINS

ZAGROS MOUNTAINS

Wheat

Making clothes

Dates

Coffee

Limes

Lemons

Tea

Making silk

Imam Mosque

Isfahan

Dates

Making clothes

Oil

IRAN

Salt Desert (Dasht-E Kavir)

Mashad

Asiatic wild ass

Barley

Cotton

Barren Desert (Dasht-E Lut)

Leopard

MOUNTAINS

AFGHANISTAN

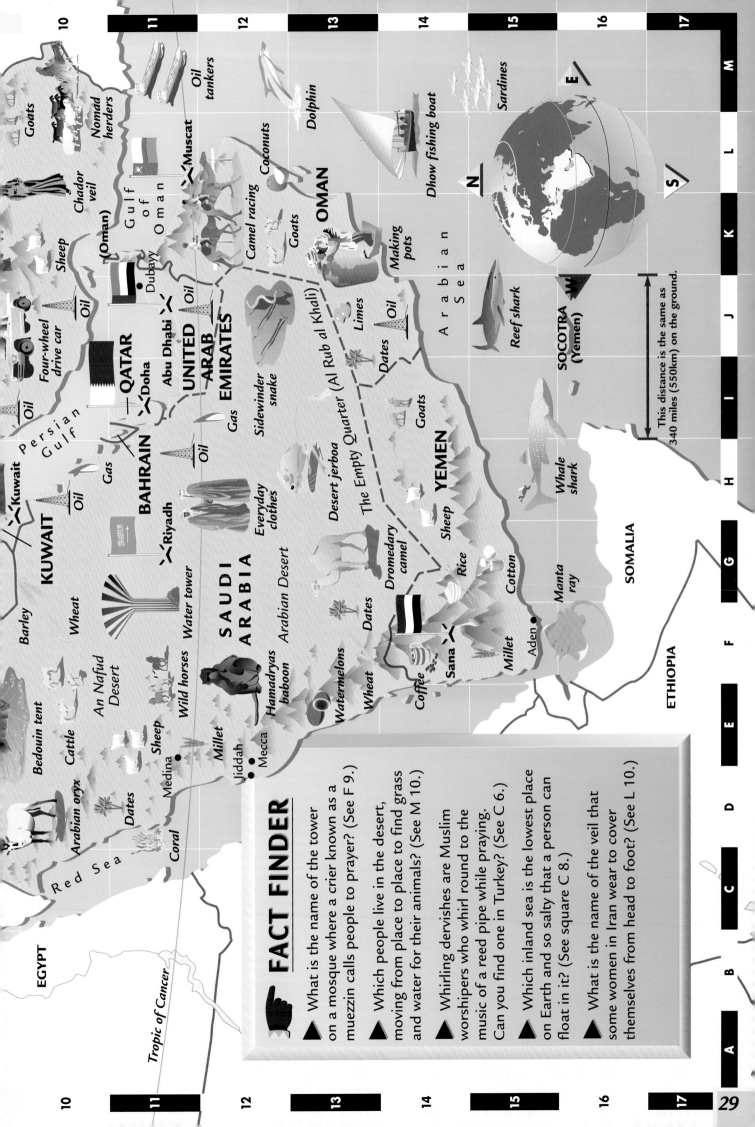

FACT FINDER

▲ What is the name of the tower on a mosque where a crier known as a muezzin calls people to prayer? (See F 9.)

▲ Which people live in the desert, moving from place to place to find grass and water for their animals? (See M 10.)

▲ Whirling dervishes are Muslim worshipers who whirl round to the music of a reed pipe while praying. Can you find one in Turkey? (See C 6.)

▲ Which inland sea is the lowest place on Earth and so salty that a person can float in it? (See square C 8.)

▲ What is the name of the veil that some women in Iran wear to cover themselves from head to foot? (See L 10.)

29

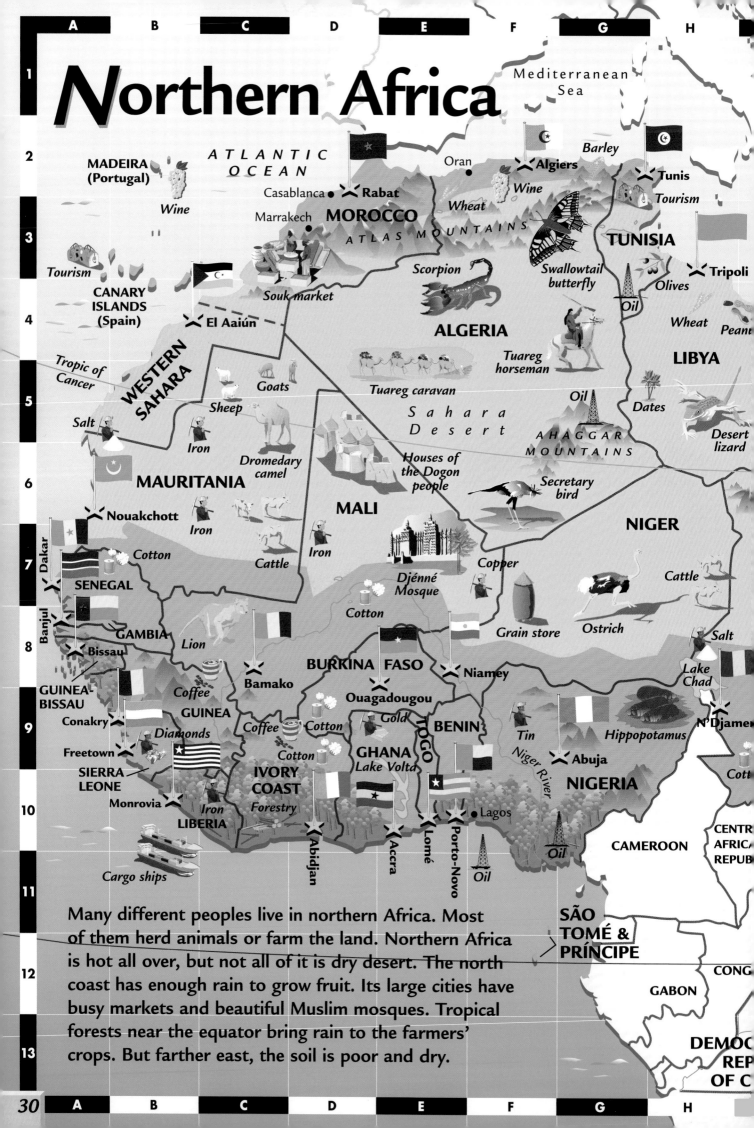

Northern Africa

Mediterranean Sea

ATLANTIC OCEAN

MADEIRA (Portugal)

Wine

Tourism

CANARY ISLANDS (Spain)

Tropic of Cancer

Salt

Casablanca • Rabat

Marrakech

MOROCCO

Souk market

El Aaiún

WESTERN SAHARA

Goats

Sheep

Iron

Dromedary camel

MAURITANIA

Nouakchott

Iron

Cattle

Dakar

Cotton

SENEGAL

Banjul

GAMBIA

Bissau

GUINEA-BISSAU

Conakry

Diamonds

Freetown

SIERRA LEONE

Monrovia

LIBERIA

Cargo ships

Lion

Coffee

GUINEA

Coffee

Iron

Forestry

IVORY COAST

Abidjan

Oran

Algiers

Wine

Wheat

ATLAS MOUNTAINS

Scorpion

ALGERIA

Tuareg caravan

Sahara Desert

Tuareg horseman

Houses of the Dogon people

MALI

Iron

Djénné Mosque

Cotton

Bamako

Cotton

Ouagadougou

BURKINA FASO

Gold

Cotton

GHANA

Lake Volta

Accra

TOGO

Lomé

BENIN

Porto-Novo

Oil

Barley

Tunis

Tourism

TUNISIA

Tripoli

Olives

Oil

Wheat

Peanu

LIBYA

Dates

Desert lizard

AHAGGAR MOUNTAINS

Oil

Secretary bird

Copper

Grain store

NIGER

Ostrich

Cattle

Salt

Lake Chad

N'Djamer

Niamey

Tin

Hippopotamus

Niger River

Abuja

NIGERIA

Lagos

Oil

SÃO TOMÉ & PRÍNCIPE

CAMEROON

CENTRAL AFRICA REPUBL

CONG

GABON

DEMOC REP OF C

Swallowtail butterfly

Many different peoples live in northern Africa. Most of them herd animals or farm the land. Northern Africa is hot all over, but not all of it is dry desert. The north coast has enough rain to grow fruit. Its large cities have busy markets and beautiful Muslim mosques. Tropical forests near the equator bring rain to the farmers' crops. But farther east, the soil is poor and dry.

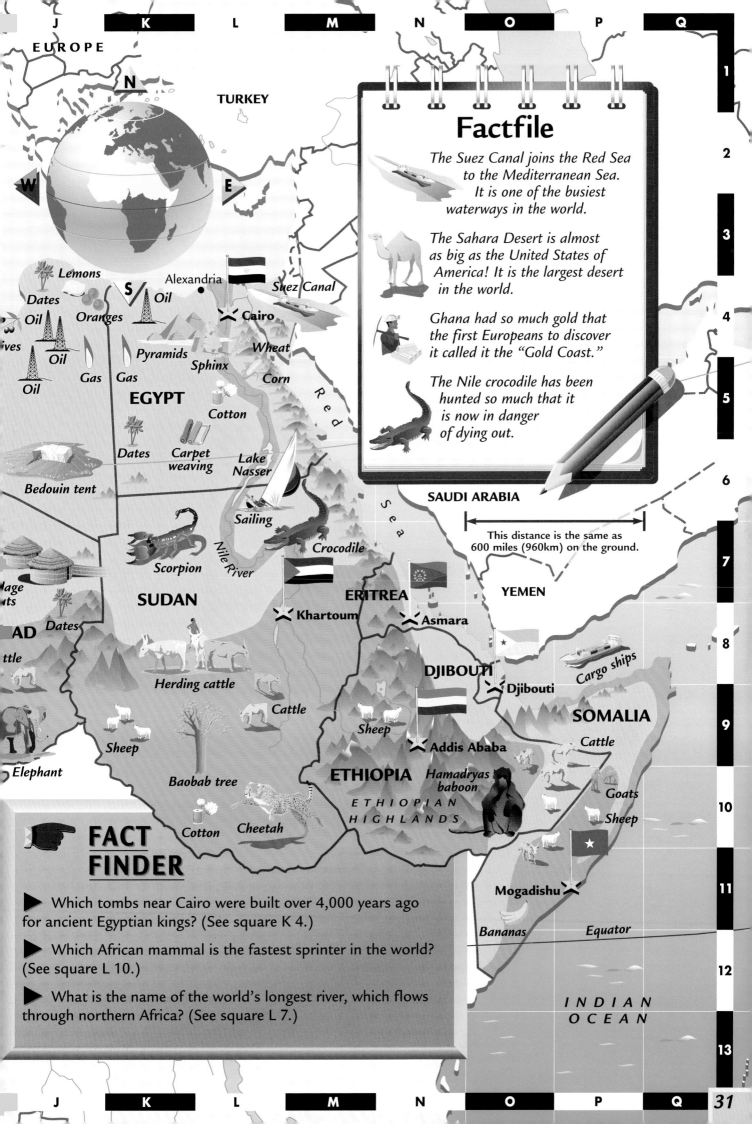

EUROPE

N

W

E

TURKEY

Factfile

The Suez Canal joins the Red Sea to the Mediterranean Sea. It is one of the busiest waterways in the world.

The Sahara Desert is almost as big as the United States of America! It is the largest desert in the world.

Ghana had so much gold that the first Europeans to discover it called it the "Gold Coast."

The Nile crocodile has been hunted so much that it is now in danger of dying out.

Lemons
Dates
Oil
Oranges
Oil
Oil
ives
Oil

S
Alexandria
Oil
Cairo

Suez Canal

Wheat

Red

Pyramids
Sphinx
Corn

Gas   Gas

EGYPT

Cotton

Dates
Carpet weaving

Lake Nasser

Bedouin tent

Sailing

Sea

SAUDI ARABIA

This distance is the same as 600 miles (960km) on the ground.

Nile River

Crocodile

Scorpion

SUDAN

Khartoum

ERITREA

Asmara

YEMEN

age ts

AD

Dates

ttle

Herding cattle

Cattle

DJIBOUTI

Djibouti

Cargo ships

SOMALIA

Cattle

Sheep

Sheep

Addis Ababa

Goats

Elephant

Baobab tree

ETHIOPIA

Hamadryas baboon

Sheep

Cotton   Cheetah

E T H I O P I A N
H I G H L A N D S

FACT FINDER

▶ Which tombs near Cairo were built over 4,000 years ago for ancient Egyptian kings? (See square K 4.)

▶ Which African mammal is the fastest sprinter in the world? (See square L 10.)

▶ What is the name of the world's longest river, which flows through northern Africa? (See square L 7.)

Mogadishu

Bananas   Equator

I N D I A N
O C E A N

Southern Africa

Southern Africa is a vast land of grasslands, rain forests, mountains, and deserts. The plains of Kenya and Tanzania are famous for their huge herds of animals. Farther west, in the rain forests, there are gorillas, monkeys, and tropical birds. Many different peoples live in Africa. Most of them farm in small villages, but the cities are growing. Many countries mine copper and gold. Some mine diamonds too.

Factfile

Southern Africa is home to the black rhino and the mountain gorilla, two of the world's most endangered animals.

Southern Africa has large areas of rain forest. Altogether, nearly one-quarter of the world's forests grow in southern Africa.

Three-quarters of the world's diamonds are mined in southern Africa.

This distance is the same as 450 miles (725km) on the ground.

Tropic of Cancer

NIGERIA

Coffee

Forestry

Yaoundé

CAMEROON

Yams

Forestry

Oil

EQUATORIAL GUINEA

Malabo

Libreville

GABON

CABINDA (Angola)

Oil

Oil

Forestry

Brazzaville

CONGO

Kinshasa

Forestry

Dug-out canoes

Kasai River

Cassava

Bangui

Diamonds

Crocodile

CENTRAL AFRICAN REPUBLIC

Forestry

Cotton

Cassava

Yams

Chimpanzee

Mountain gorilla

Congo River

Okapi

DEMOCRATIC REPUBLIC OF CONGO

Diamonds

CHAD

SUDAN

ETHIOPIA

SOMALIA

Coffee

Coffee

UGANDA

Kampala

Lake Victoria

Flamingos

KENYA

Nairobi

Office blocks

Coffee

Tea

Mt. Kilimanjaro

Tourism

Zanzibar Island

Kigali

RWANDA

Bujumbura

BURUNDI

Lake Tanganyika

Elephants

Balloon

Dodoma

Dar es

Equator

Mountain gorilla

SEYCHELLES

N

S

E

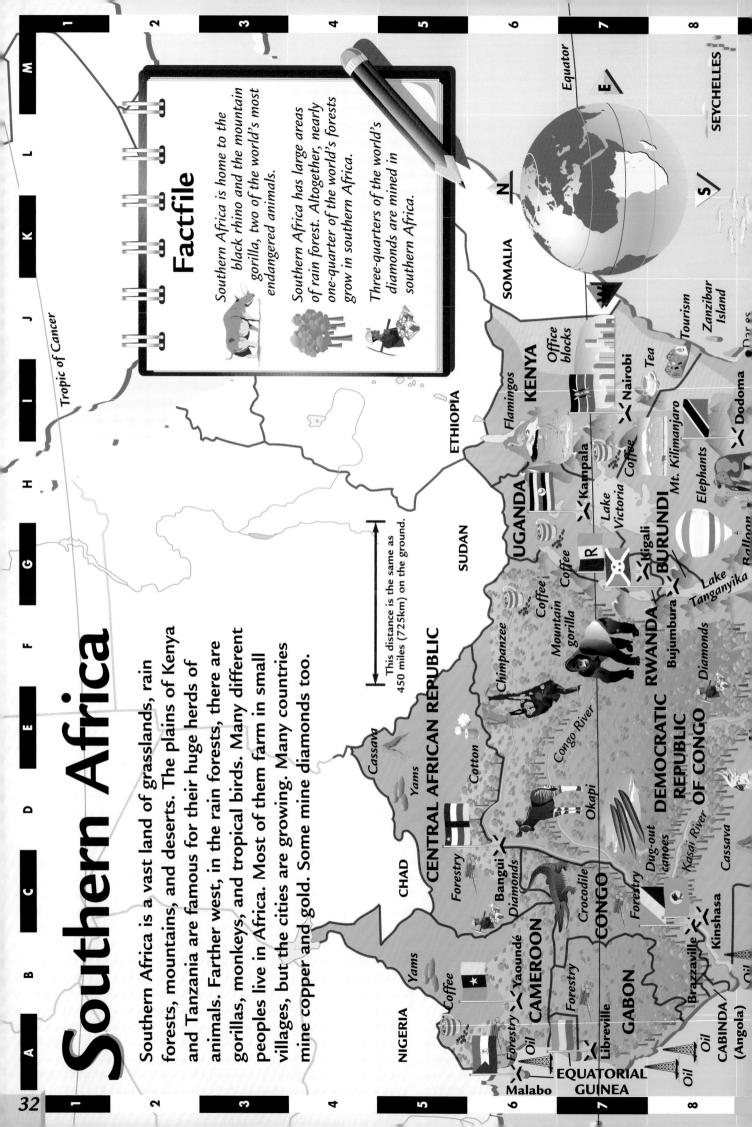

FACT FINDER

▲ What is the name of the largest lake in Africa and the second largest freshwater lake in the world? (See square H 7.)

▲ Which African mountain is close to the equator, but is so high that it is always covered in snow? (See square H 8.)

▲ Which African tree can store more than five hundred bathtubs of water in its trunk? (See square K 14.)

COMOROS

Teardrop butterfly fish

MAYOTTE (France)

Millet

Sugar cane

Polka dot grouper fish

Chameleon

MADAGASCAR

Coffee

Antananarivo

Rice

Bananas

Shrimp

Sea horses

MAURITIUS

REUNION (France)

Ring-tailed lemur

Baobab tree

Herding cattle

Forestry

MALAWI

Lake Nyasa

Coffee

Lilongwe

Farming with hand tools

Cashew nuts

Cotton

Humpback whale

MOZAMBIQUE

Giraffe

Copper

ZAMBIA

Copper

Tobacco

Diamonds

Lusaka

Tobacco

Gold

Victoria Falls

Harare

ZIMBABWE

Ruins of Great Zimbabwe

Cotton

Maputo

Mbabane

SWAZILAND

LESOTHO

Maseru

Cargo ships

Durban

Lobster

Cargo ships

Cargo ships

Zambezi River

Hippopotamus

Diamonds

Gold

Pretoria

Johannesburg

Gold

Coal

Corn

Diamonds

Gold

Apples

Cattle

REPUBLIC OF SOUTH AFRICA

Wine

Oranges

Cape of Good Hope

Black rhino

Coffee

Luanda

Cargo ships

ATLANTIC OCEAN

ANGOLA

Diamonds

Lion

Village of Ovambo people

Weaverbird

NAMIBIA

Windhoek

Meerkats

Kalahari Desert

Gaborone

BOTSWANA

Cattle

Cattle

Orange River

Ostrich

Cape Town

Table Mountain

Namib Desert

Welwitschia plant

Diamonds

Cattle

Tropic of Capricorn

Anchovies

Right whale

Cargo ships

Southern Asia

Southern Asia stretches from the Himalaya in the north of India to the island of Sri Lanka in the south. The weather is mostly hot and dry, although for several months of the year there are heavy rains. More than a billion people live in southern Asia. Most people live in villages and farm the land, but many are beginning to move to the cities. The cities are a mixture of old and new, with modern buildings next to ancient temples and palaces. The busy streets are packed with cars, trucks and buses, but also with bullock carts and elephants.

👉 FACT FINDER

▲ Which white marble temple, decorated with precious stones, was built in the 17th century by an Indian emperor as a burial place for his wife? (See square G 8.)

▲ In India, which animal is used to help people with heavy work such as moving timber? (See square F 11.)

▲ What are Pakistan, Afghanistan, and India all famous for weaving? (See squares C 6, C 9 and F 7.)

▲ In India, which three-wheeled vehicle that looks a little like a bicycle is often used to carry people from one place to another? (See square I 10.)

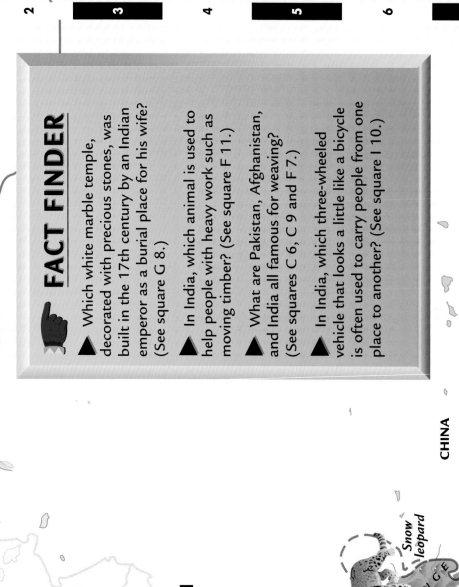

TURKMENISTAN

UZBEKISTAN

TAJIKISTAN

CHINA

Blue Mosque

Cattle

Carpet weaving

Kabul

Bactrian camel

Milking goats

AFGHANISTAN

Cotton

Helmand River

Wheat

Rubies

Peaches

Goats

Quetta

PAKISTAN

Cotton

Wheat

Indus River

Thar

Cobra

Sugar cane

Lahore

Wheat

Shah Faisal Mosque

Islamabad

KARAKORAM

RANGE

Snow leopard

Carpet weaving

Wheat

Cattle

Goats

New Delhi

HIMALAYA

Mountain peaks

Yak

NEPAL

Kathmandu

Sugar

Mt. Everest

Tea

Thimphu

BHUTAN

Brahmaputra River

Tea

Oil

Buddhist monk

Indian rhino

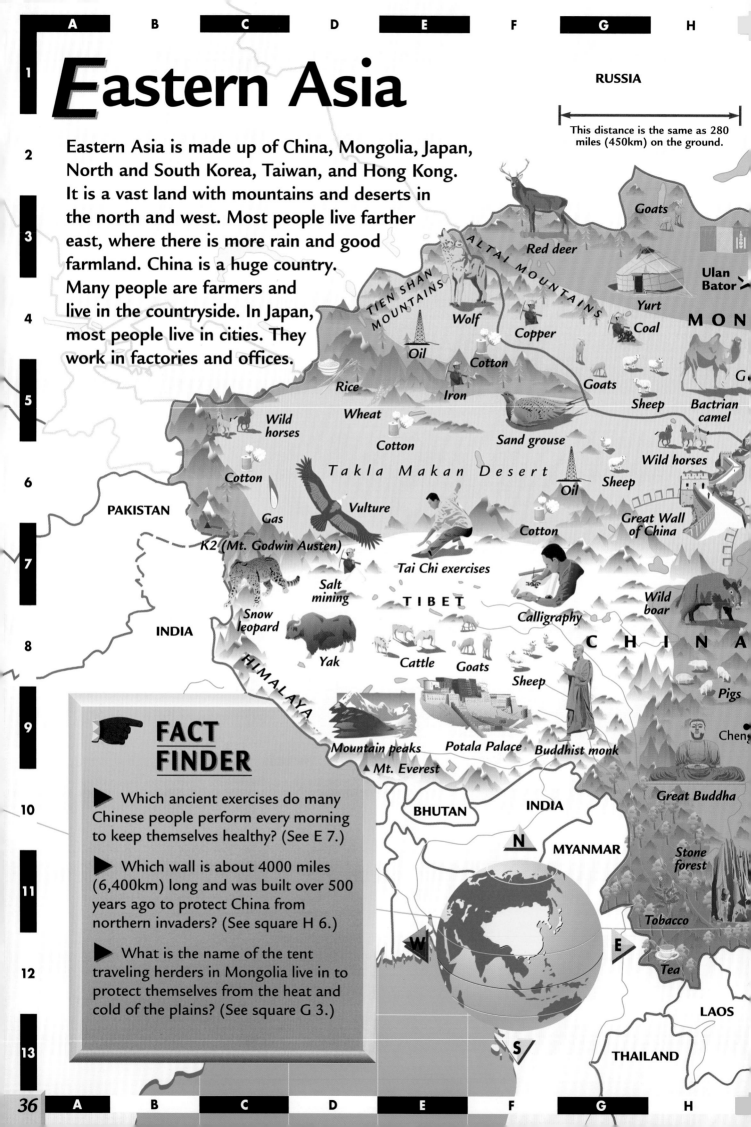

Eastern Asia

Eastern Asia is made up of China, Mongolia, Japan, North and South Korea, Taiwan, and Hong Kong. It is a vast land with mountains and deserts in the north and west. Most people live farther east, where there is more rain and good farmland. China is a huge country. Many people are farmers and live in the countryside. In Japan, most people live in cities. They work in factories and offices.

RUSSIA

This distance is the same as 280 miles (450km) on the ground.

ALTAI MOUNTAINS
TIEN SHAN MOUNTAINS

Red deer
Goats
Wolf
Copper
Coal
Yurt
Ulan Bator
M O N
Oil
Cotton
Rice
Iron
Wheat
Goats
Sheep
Bactrian camel
Wild horses
Cotton
Sand grouse
Takla Makan Desert
Cotton
Gas
Vulture
Oil
Sheep
Wild horses
Great Wall of China
K2 (Mt. Godwin Austen)
Tai Chi exercises
PAKISTAN
Salt mining
T I B E T
Calligraphy
Wild boar
Snow leopard
C H I N A
INDIA
Yak
Cattle
Goats
Sheep
Pigs
HIMALAYA
Mountain peaks
Potala Palace
Buddhist monk
Cheng
▲ Mt. Everest
Great Buddha
BHUTAN
INDIA
Stone forest
N
MYANMAR
Tobacco
W
E
Tea
LAOS
S
THAILAND

FACT FINDER

▶ Which ancient exercises do many Chinese people perform every morning to keep themselves healthy? (See E 7.)

▶ Which wall is about 4000 miles (6,400km) long and was built over 500 years ago to protect China from northern invaders? (See square H 6.)

▶ What is the name of the tent traveling herders in Mongolia live in to protect themselves from the heat and cold of the plains? (See square G 3.)

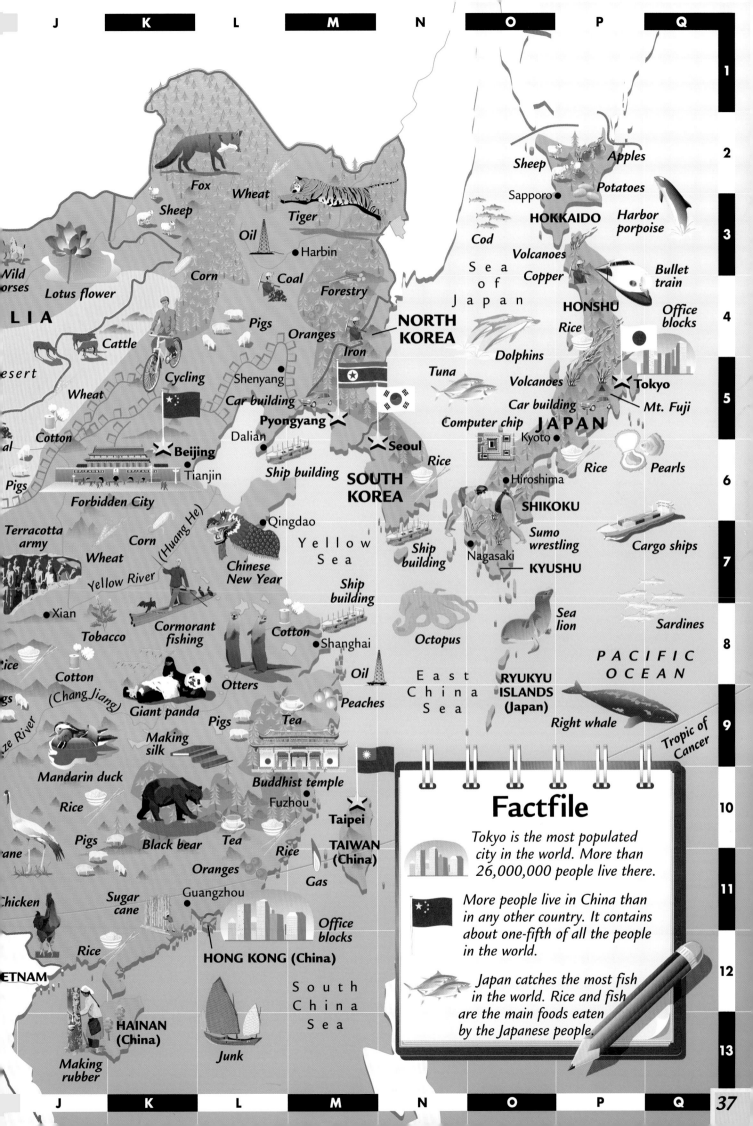

Fox
Wheat
Sheep
Tiger
Oil
Harbin
Corn
Coal
Forestry
Pigs
Oranges
Iron
Wild horses
Lotus flower
LIA
Cattle
Cycling
Wheat
Cotton
al
Pigs
Shenyang
Car building
Pyongyang
Dalian
Beijing
Tianjin
Forbidden City
Terracotta army
Corn
(Huang He)
Wheat
Yellow River
Chinese New Year
Qingdao
Yellow Sea
Xian
Tobacco
Cormorant fishing
Cotton
Shanghai
ice
Cotton
(Chang Jiang)
Giant panda
Pigs
Making silk
Otters
Tea
Oil
Peaches
gs
Mandarin duck
Rice
Pigs
Black bear
Tea
Buddhist temple
Fuzhou
Oranges
Taipei
ane
Chicken
Sugar cane
Guangzhou
Rice
Gas
Office blocks
TAIWAN (China)
Rice
HONG KONG (China)
ETNAM
HAINAN (China)
Making rubber
Junk
South China Sea

NORTH KOREA
Seoul
SOUTH KOREA
Rice
Ship building
Ship building
Ship building
Octopus
East China Sea

Sheep
Apples
Sapporo
Potatoes
HOKKAIDO
Harbor porpoise
Cod
Volcanoes
Sea of Japan
Copper
Bullet train
HONSHU
Rice
Office blocks
Dolphins
Tuna
Volcanoes
Tokyo
Car building
Mt. Fuji
Computer chip
JAPAN
Kyoto
Rice
Pearls
Hiroshima
SHIKOKU
Sumo wrestling
Cargo ships
Nagasaki
KYUSHU
Sea lion
Sardines
PACIFIC OCEAN
RYUKYU ISLANDS (Japan)
Right whale
Tropic of Cancer

Factfile

Tokyo is the most populated city in the world. More than 26,000,000 people live there.

More people live in China than in any other country. It contains about one-fifth of all the people in the world.

Japan catches the most fish in the world. Rice and fish are the main foods eaten by the Japanese people.

Southeast Asia

TAIWAN

Scuba diving

CHINA

Tropic of Cancer

Coal

Clown fish

Coral

Stilt house

Wild boar

MYANMAR

Water buffalo

Hanoi

South China Sea

LUZON

Coral

Copper

Manila

Working elephant

LAOS

Cargo ships

Rice

Tiger

Vientiane

THAILAND

VIETNAM

PHILI

Making silk

Mekong River

Irrawaddy River

Herring

Coral

Silver

Floating market

Rice

Cassava

Anchovies

Gold

Yangon

Sardines

Bangkok

Corn

INDIAN OCEAN

Angkor Wat

Ho Chi Minh City

Phnom Penh

Pearls

Oil

CAMBODIA

Rice

Tuna

BRUNEI

Bandar Seri Begawan

Reef sharks

Gas

Oil

Making rubber

Leatherback turtle

Rice

Lobster

Tourism

MALAYSIA

Polka dot grouper fish

Malayan tapir

Iron

Forestry

Orang-utan

Coral

Office blocks

Tourism

SINGAPORE

BORNEO

Oil

Kuala Lumpur

Volcanoes

Oil

Forestry

IND

SUMATRA

Cargo ships

Gas

Orchi

Volcanoes

Rafflesia flower

Jakarta JAVA

Volcanoe

Tea

Sea horses

Teardrop butterfly fis.

Coral

👉 FACT FINDER

▶ What is the name of the world's largest lizard? It can grow more than 10 feet (3m) long and lives only in Indonesia. (See square J 11.)

▶ Which temple in Cambodia is one of the architectural wonders of the world? It was built over 800 years ago to honor the Hindu god, Vishnu. (See square D 7.)

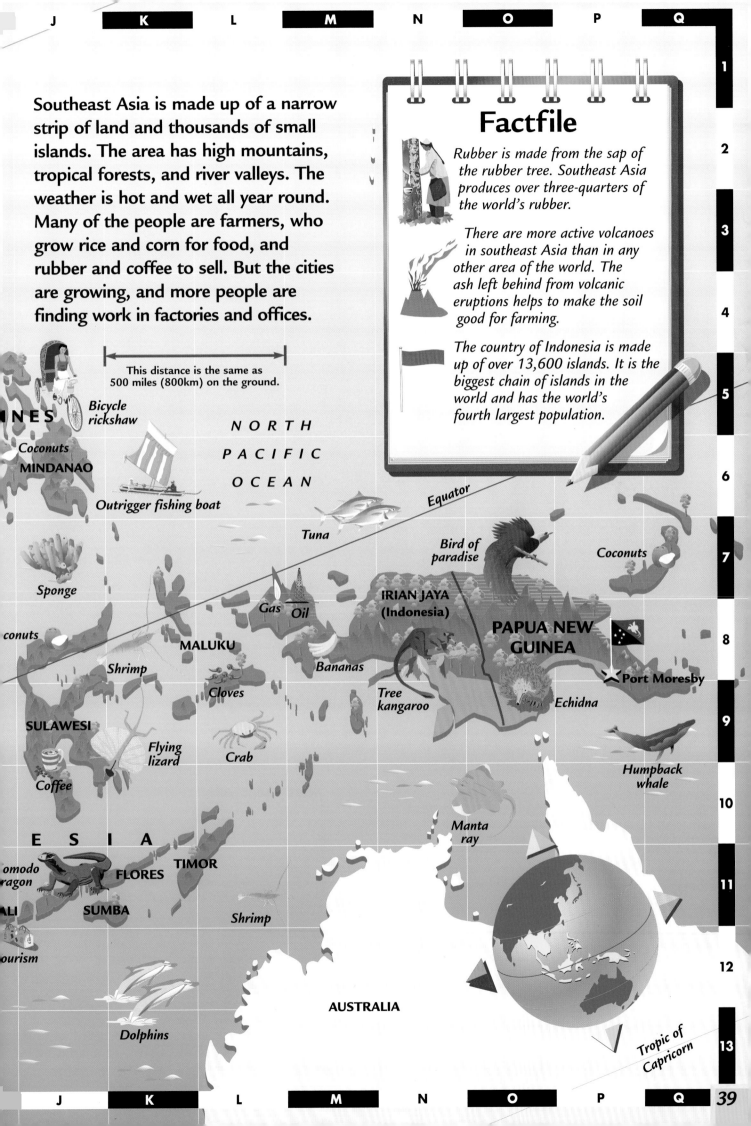

Southeast Asia is made up of a narrow strip of land and thousands of small islands. The area has high mountains, tropical forests, and river valleys. The weather is hot and wet all year round. Many of the people are farmers, who grow rice and corn for food, and rubber and coffee to sell. But the cities are growing, and more people are finding work in factories and offices.

This distance is the same as 500 miles (800km) on the ground.

Factfile

Rubber is made from the sap of the rubber tree. Southeast Asia produces over three-quarters of the world's rubber.

There are more active volcanoes in southeast Asia than in any other area of the world. The ash left behind from volcanic eruptions helps to make the soil good for farming.

The country of Indonesia is made up of over 13,600 islands. It is the biggest chain of islands in the world and has the world's fourth largest population.

Bicycle rickshaw

NES

Coconuts
MINDANAO

N O R T H

P A C I F I C

O C E A N

Outrigger fishing boat

Tuna

Equator

Sponge

Bird of paradise

Coconuts

conuts

Gas   Oil

IRIAN JAYA (Indonesia)

PAPUA NEW GUINEA

MALUKU

Shrimp

Bananas

Cloves

Tree kangaroo

Port Moresby

Echidna

SULAWESI

Flying lizard

Crab

Humpback whale

Coffee

E S I A

omodo ragon

TIMOR

FLORES

Manta ray

ALI

SUMBA

Shrimp

ourism

AUSTRALIA

Dolphins

Tropic of Capricorn

Australia, New Zealand, and the Pacific Islands

The Pacific Ocean is dotted with thousands of islands. Many people live in villages and grow crops or hunt for fish. Australia is an island too, but it is so big that it is a continent. Most Australians live in cities or farm land near the coast. A lot of Australia is hot and dry, but it has mountains and rain forests too. It also has animals and plants that are not found anywhere else.

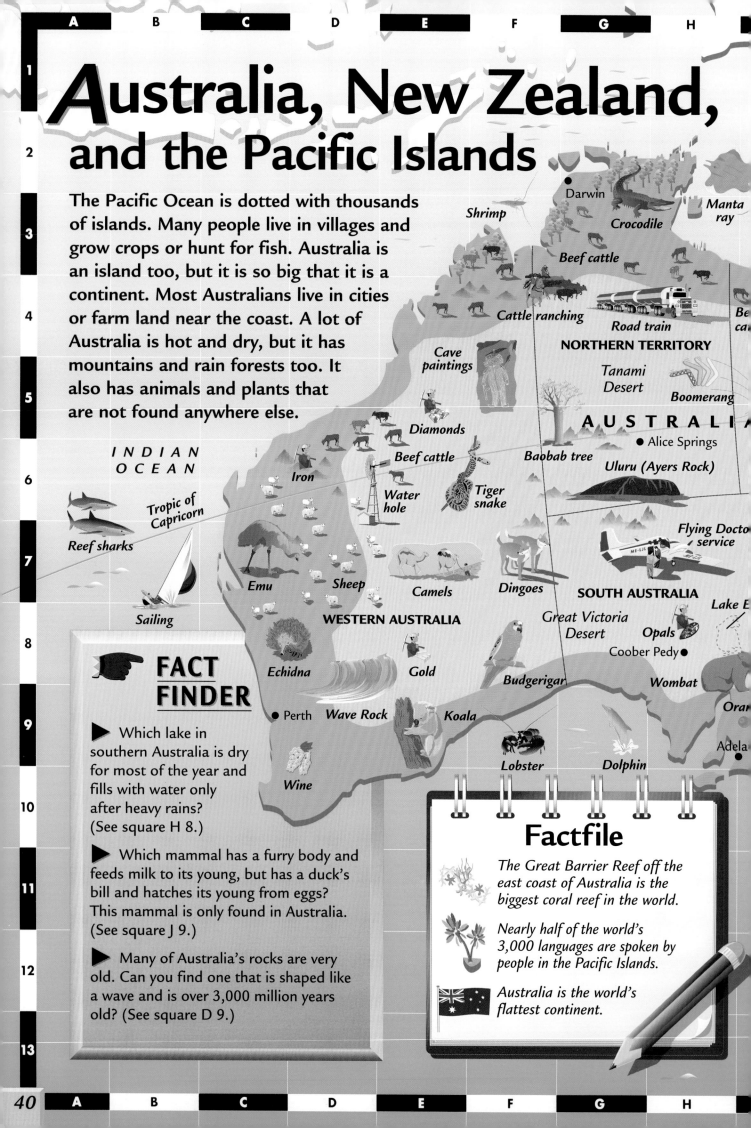

Darwin

Shrimp

Crocodile

Manta ray

Beef cattle

Cattle ranching

Road train

Be ca

NORTHERN TERRITORY

Cave paintings

Tanami Desert

Boomerang

A U S T R A L I A

Diamonds

Iron

Beef cattle

Baobab tree

● Alice Springs

Uluru (Ayers Rock)

Water hole

Tiger snake

INDIAN OCEAN

Tropic of Capricorn

Reef sharks

Flying Docto service

Emu

Sheep

Camels

Dingoes

SOUTH AUSTRALIA

Lake E

Sailing

WESTERN AUSTRALIA

Great Victoria Desert

Opals

Coober Pedy ●

Echidna

Gold

Budgerigar

Wombat

● Perth

Wave Rock

Koala

Orar

Lobster

Dolphin

Adela

Wine

FACT FINDER

▶ Which lake in southern Australia is dry for most of the year and fills with water only after heavy rains? (See square H 8.)

▶ Which mammal has a furry body and feeds milk to its young, but has a duck's bill and hatches its young from eggs? This mammal is only found in Australia. (See square J 9.)

▶ Many of Australia's rocks are very old. Can you find one that is shaped like a wave and is over 3,000 million years old? (See square D 9.)

Factfile

The Great Barrier Reef off the east coast of Australia is the biggest coral reef in the world.

Nearly half of the world's 3,000 languages are spoken by people in the Pacific Islands.

Australia is the world's flattest continent.

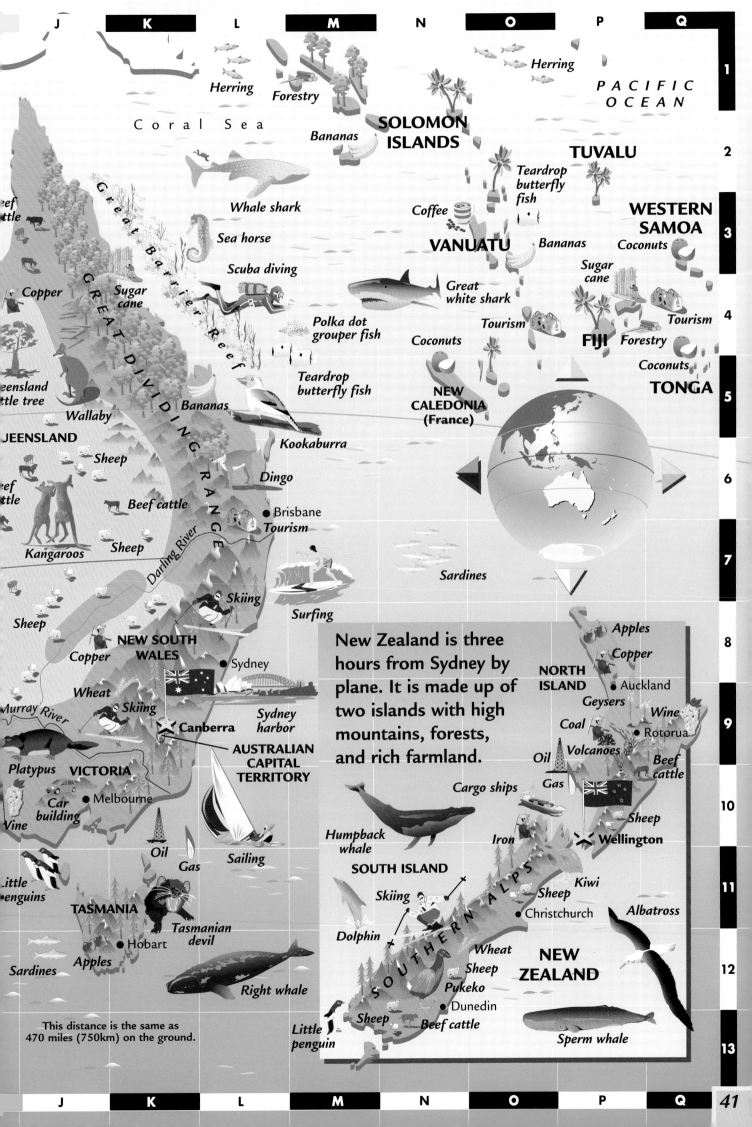

Map Labels

J K L M N O P Q
1 2 3 4 5 6 7 8 9 10 11 12 13

PACIFIC OCEAN

Herring

Forestry

Herring

C o r a l   S e a

SOLOMON ISLANDS

Bananas

TUVALU

Whale shark

Teardrop butterfly fish

WESTERN SAMOA

Sea horse

Coffee

Coconuts

Scuba diving

VANUATU

Bananas

Sugar cane

Copper

Sugar cane

GREAT BARRIER REEF

GREAT DIVIDING RANGE

Great white shark

Polka dot grouper fish

Tourism

Coconuts

Tourism

Queensland bottle tree

Teardrop butterfly fish

Coconuts

FIJI

Forestry

Wallaby

Bananas

NEW CALEDONIA (France)

TONGA

QUEENSLAND

Kookaburra

Sheep

Dingo

Beef cattle

Beef cattle

Brisbane

Tourism

Sardines

Kangaroos

Sheep

Sheep

Darling River

Skiing

Surfing

Apples

Copper

NORTH ISLAND

Sheep

NEW SOUTH WALES

Sydney

New Zealand is three hours from Sydney by plane. It is made up of two islands with high mountains, forests, and rich farmland.

Auckland

Geysers

Wine

Copper

Murray River

Wheat

Skiing

Coal

Rotorua

Canberra

Sydney harbor

Volcanoes

Oil

Beef cattle

AUSTRALIAN CAPITAL TERRITORY

Gas

Platypus

VICTORIA

Cargo ships

Sheep

Car building

Melbourne

Humpback whale

Iron

Wellington

Vine

Oil

Gas

Sailing

SOUTH ISLAND

SOUTHERN ALPS

Kiwi

Sheep

Albatross

Little penguins

Christchurch

TASMANIA

Tasmanian devil

Skiing

Wheat

NEW ZEALAND

Hobart

Dolphin

Sheep

Sardines

Apples

Pukeko

Right whale

Dunedin

This distance is the same as 470 miles (750km) on the ground.

Little penguin

Sheep

Beef cattle

Sperm whale

41

Fascinating facts

On these pages, you can discover interesting facts about the world. Look up the names of the places in the index and find out where they are on the maps in this atlas.

Where in the world is...

...the hottest place?
Al Aziziyah in Libya. The highest temperature ever recorded was 136°F (58°C).

In Al Aziziyah, you could fry an egg on a sun-baked rock.

...the coldest place?
Vostock in Antarctica. The lowest temperature ever recorded was -129°F. (-89°C). This is over three times as cold as inside a deep freeze.

...the wettest place? Mawsynram in India, where nearly 40 feet (12m) of rain falls each year. This is enough to cover a three-story building.

...the driest place? Atacama Desert in Chile, where it has rained only a few times in the last 400 years.

Which country is the...

...biggest country?
Russia, which is 6,592,850 square miles (17,075,400sq km).

...smallest country?
Vatican City, which is 109 acres (44 hectares).

If Russia were the size of a soccer field, the Vatican City would be the size of a small stamp.

...emptiest country?
Mongolia, which has a huge desert and towering mountains. There are only a few towns which are far apart.

...most crowded country?
Monaco, which is a tiny country in Europe. It has an orchestra larger than its army.

Where is the...

...highest mountain in the world?
Mount Everest in the Himalaya, in Nepal. It is about 29,028 ft. (8,848m) high—over nine times as tall as the highest waterfall in the world.

29,028 feet

...highest waterfall in the world?
Angel Falls, in Venezuela. It has a total drop of about 3,212 ft. (979m)—over twice as high as the tallest building in North America.

3,212 feet

...highest geyser in the world?
Waimangu Geyser, in New Zealand. It once shot out a jet of water 1,510 ft. (460m) high—slightly taller than Sears Tower.

1,510 feet

...highest building in North America?
Sears Tower, US. It is about 1,454 ft. (443m) tall—nearly four times taller than the tallest tree in the world.

1,454 feet

...highest tree in the world?
A redwood tree in California, US. It is about 368 ft. (112m) high—over 40 times taller than the tallest person in the world.

368 feet

Who was the world's tallest person?
An American called Robert Pershing Wadlow was the world's tallest person. He was over 8 ft., 11 in. (2.7m) tall.

FACT FINDER

Find these record-breaking places in the atlas

▶ The highest mountain (page 34, square J 8

▶ The tallest waterfall (page 20, square E 4)

▶ The longest river (page 31, square L 7)

▶ The driest place (page 21, square E 9)

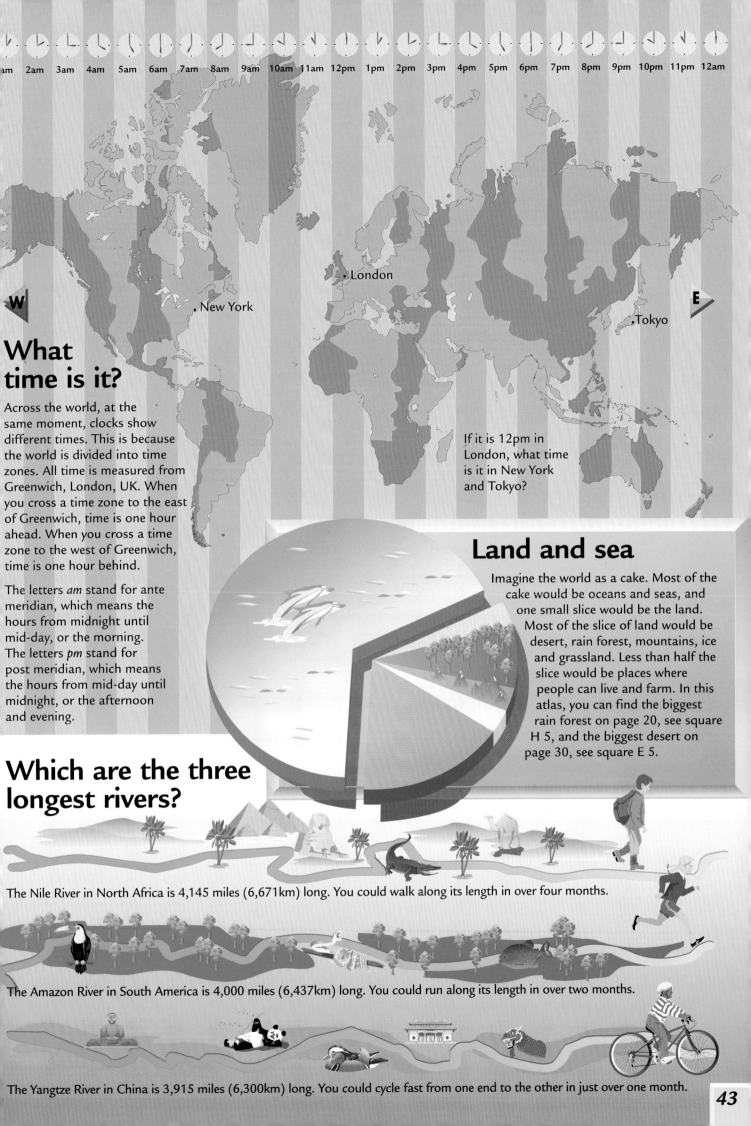

W

E

.London

.New York

.Tokyo

What time is it?

Across the world, at the same moment, clocks show different times. This is because the world is divided into time zones. All time is measured from Greenwich, London, UK. When you cross a time zone to the east of Greenwich, time is one hour ahead. When you cross a time zone to the west of Greenwich, time is one hour behind.

The letters *am* stand for ante meridian, which means the hours from midnight until mid-day, or the morning. The letters *pm* stand for post meridian, which means the hours from mid-day until midnight, or the afternoon and evening.

If it is 12pm in London, what time is it in New York and Tokyo?

Land and sea

Imagine the world as a cake. Most of the cake would be oceans and seas, and one small slice would be the land. Most of the slice of land would be desert, rain forest, mountains, ice and grassland. Less than half the slice would be places where people can live and farm. In this atlas, you can find the biggest rain forest on page 20, see square H 5, and the biggest desert on page 30, see square E 5.

Which are the three longest rivers?

The Nile River in North Africa is 4,145 miles (6,671km) long. You could walk along its length in over four months.

The Amazon River in South America is 4,000 miles (6,437km) long. You could run along its length in over two months.

The Yangtze River in China is 3,915 miles (6,300km) long. You could cycle fast from one end to the other in just over one month.

43

Index

This index lists all the places on the maps in this atlas. The page number tells you which map to go to and the grid reference tells you where the place is on the map. You can find out how to use grid references on page 9.

*T*roubleshooting tips

System requirements

The Atlas disk will work on most Windows or Apple Macintosh computers.
To check that it will run on yours, please read the minimum specifications below.

- ### Windows
  486DX2/66Mhz PC with Windows version 3.1, 3.11, 95 or 98; VGA color
  monitor; SoundBlaster-compatible soundcard; 8Mb RAM (16Mb RAM
  recommended with Windows 95; 24 Mb recommended with Windows 98).

- ### Macintosh
  Apple Macintosh with 68020 processor (or Power Macintosh), system 7.0
  (or later) and 16Mb of RAM (24 Mb with Power Macintosh).

Quick fixes

To get the most out of your Atlas disk, please check:
1. Your monitor is set to 640 x 480 and 256 colors.
2. You have the Arial font (Windows users) or Helvetica font (Macintosh users)
installed in your fonts folder.
3. You have no other applications open.

Read me file

If you have a problem with your Atlas disk that is not covered in the notes above,
be sure to check the Read me file. You can open the Read me file by clicking on
the Read me icon which you will find next to the Atlas icon.

Helpline

If you come across a problem loading or running the Atlas disk, you should find
the solution here. If you still cannot solve your problem, call the helpline at
1-609-921-6700. Remember to get permission from the person who pays the bill
before you use the phone.

Published in the United States
and Canada by
Two-Can Publishing LLC
234 Nassau Street
Princeton, NJ 08542

www.two-canpublishing.com

© 2000 Two-Can Publishing

For information on other Two-Can books and
multimedia, call 1-609-921-6700,
fax 1-609-921-3349, or visit our web site at
http://www.two-canpublishing.com

Created by
act-two
346 Old Street
London EC1V 9RB

Disk
Creative Director: Jason Page
Programming Director: Paul Steven
Art Director: Sarah Evans
Senior Designer: James Evans
Editors: Rob Mitchell, Lyndall Thomas
Programmer: Roger Emery
Authors: Jason Page, Rob Mitchell,
Lyndall Thomas, Lucy Arnold
Illustrators: Jon Stuart, James Jarvis,
Mel Pickering
Production Director: Lorraine Estelle
Production Controller: KatherineHarvey
Project Manager: Joya Bart-Plange

Book
Text: Andrew Solway
Consultant: Steve Watts
Computer Illustrations: Mel Pickering,
Jacqueline Land
Editors: Deborah Kespert, Kate Asser,
Editoral Support: Claire Llewellyn,
Julia Hillyard, Claire Yude
Art Director: Belinda Webster
Senior Designer: Helen Holmes
Designer: Michele Egar

All rights reserved. No part of this publication
may be reproduced, stored in a retrieval
system or transmitted in any form or by any
means electronic, mechanical, photocopying,
recording or otherwise, without prior written
permission of the publisher.

'Two-Can' and 'Interfact' are trademarks of
Two-Can Publishing .

Two-Can Publishing is a division of
Zenith Entertainment plc,
43-45 Dorset Street, London W1H 4AB

1 2 3 4 5 6 7 8 9 10 04 03 02 01 00

Photographic Credits: ZEFA: p7;
John Englefield: p9

Printed in Hong Kong

CHECK OUT THE WHOLE INTERFACT RANGE

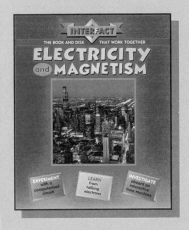

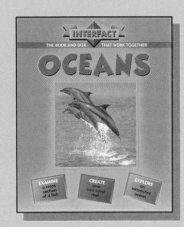

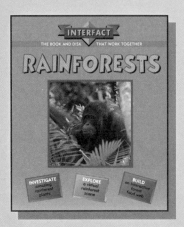

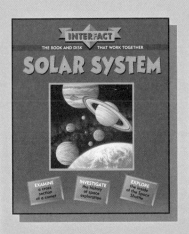

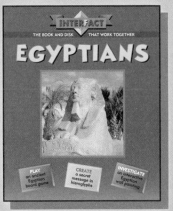

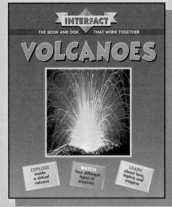

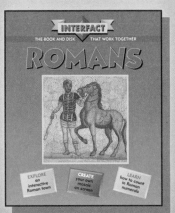

There is a huge range of
INTERFACT titles to choose from.
Watch out for new titles too!